Exchange Rates and International Financial Markets

This book poses the important question of whether exchange rates are ultimately tied down by economic fundamentals. In a unique approach, the subject is analyzed from an asset holder's perspective and Streissler takes the reader through an authoritative and wide-ranging study including:

- Friedman's case for flexible exchange rates
- interest parity and purchasing power parity
- process analysis of temporal exchange rate equilibria
- stabilization through bounded interest rates and exchange rate theory
- the problem of the neutrality of money.

Erich W. Streissler's series of lectures is cleverly presented and informative about this particularly dynamic field of research. Indispensable to advanced students and academics alike, *Exchange Rates and International Financial Markets* will also be of great interest to economic policy makers.

Erich W. Streissler was Treasurer of the International Economic Association and is a professor at the University of Vienna.

The Graz Schumpeter Lectures

1 Evolutionary Economics and Creative Destruction
J. Stanley Metcalfe

2 Knowledge, Institutions and Evolution in Economics
Brian J. Loasby

3 Schumpeter and the Endogeneity of Technology
Some American perspectives
Nathan Rosenberg

4 Consumption Takes Time
Implications for economic theory
Ian Steedman

5 Exchange Rates and International Financial Markets
An asset-theoretic perspective with Schumpeterian innovation
Erich W. Streissler

Exchange Rates and International Financial Markets

An asset-theoretic perspective with Schumpeterian innovation

Erich W. Streissler

London and New York

First published 2002
by Routledge
11 New Fetter Lane, London EC4P 4EE

Simultaneously published in the USA and Canada
by Routledge
29 West 35th Street, New York, NY 10001

Routledge is an imprint of the Taylor & Francis Group

Typeset in Times by Wearset Ltd, Boldon, Tyne and Wear
Printed and bound in Great Britain by MPG Books Ltd, Bodmin

British Library Cataloguing in Publication Data
A catalogue record for this book is available from the British Library

Library of Congress Cataloging in Publication Data
Streissler, Erich W., 1933–
Exchange rates and international financial markets : an asset-theoretic perspective with Schumpeterian innovation / Erich W. Streissler.
p. cm. — (The Graz Schumpeter lectures)
Includes bibliographical references and index
1. Foreign exchange rates. 2. International finance. I. Title.
II. Series

HG3821 .S77 2002
332.4'56–dc21

2001051063

ISBN 0-415-27746-9

Contents

Lecture I Fundamentals?

Exchange rates in the light of Schumpeter, but not of Diocletian

Introductory survey

'One of the most controversial issues in the international literature concerns the role of economic fundamentals in explaining exchange rate behaviour.'[1] 'Are exchange rates ultimately tied down by economic fundamentals, or are they free to drift at random on a sea of speculation?'[2] These are, respectively, the opening sentences of two articles in a quite recent survey on exchange rates conducted by the *Economic Journal*. And the remaining two articles in the series basically assume that for exchange rates no 'economic fundamentals' in the conventional sense can be found. The question of whether 'fundamentals' exist for such a central price as the exchange rate is, indeed, a 'fundamental' question for economic reasoning as such.

But perhaps the problem is posed incorrectly. Perhaps the quest for exchange rate 'fundamentals' is only a symptom of the application of a wrong price-theoretic paradigm altogether. Why should there be, in the conventional sense, any 'fundamentals' for an asset price (and the exchange rate is an asset price)? The assumption that there should be one we shall call the assumption of (the Emperor) Diocletian. Whether he was right in thinking that there is something like a *pretium verum* – and that its existence even makes it a *pretium iustum* – will be our first basic topic.

To question this is very much in the spirit of Joseph A. Schumpeter – and, in a slightly different sense, also in the spirit of Friedrich A. von Hayek. In other words, it is a very 'Austrian' question. It has not been sufficiently realized, perhaps, that Schumpeter in his vision of the creative entrepreneur assumes that there is no rationally determinable price for innovations, that innovations have no *pretium verum*, no true price in the sense of the Emperor Diocletian. Is this true only for innovations? And what are innovations anyhow? These will be our next questions.

If there is no true price – or, as economists have put it ever since Adam Smith, no *natural price* – for exchange rates, we have to rethink the whole of exchange rate theory. We have to rethink exchange rates, perhaps the most important subspecies of prices of the types of assets to which internationally traded moneys belong. This will be the third topic, and the most exhaustively treated of these lectures.

Exchange rates are the *relative prices of moneys*. Evidently, they have monetary causes. But if they do not have a price which is determined by fundamentals in the customary sense, then a further pillar of economic thought begins to totter: the 'non-neutrality' of exchange rates is the most important reason for the non-neutrality of money even in the long run. That will be our fourth and last topic.

Basically, the subject will be regarded in an asset-theoretic approach or, more precisely, from an asset holder's perspective. Our thinking about exchange rates is somewhat flawed from the outset: they tend to be conceived as, at base, nothing but veils covering the relative pricing of two flows of commodities, exports and imports – and that, in spite of copious evidence that such a conception is empirically untenable, at least up to a very long medium run. If only two or even only one per cent of exchange rate transactions nowadays are due to the purchase or sale of such commodities and 98 or 99 per cent due to some kind of capital transaction, how can commodity market pricing alone be expected to determine exchange rates? It is therefore important to understand exchange rates as what they are at their face value: the price of one national currency against another, a relative price of moneys. 'Money is one kind of asset, one way of holding wealth,'[3] as the founder of modern monetarism famously remarked, though not taking his own dictum too seriously himself. The asset '(foreign) money' can be held for its own sake, because of its expected appreciation against another kind of money. Or money may be exchanged for other goods; but in internationally integrated capital markets the purchase of current commodity flows will be its least important first-round use. Much rather, it will be exchanged for other assets, for credit instruments, stocks and shares, for real estate, or for direct investments in firms. In this sense the exchange rate, as viewed by asset holders, is perhaps best described as a relative *double asset price*: the price of the asset 'foreign money', most likely to be exchanged, and conditioned by, investment opportunities in other assets of that currency area. Foreign exchange is an asset for buying other assets. Such a double asset price may be a well-determined and stable price due to stabilizing expectations and stabilizing institutions of exchange. But there is no reason whatsoever why this has to be so. And in uncertain times such double asset prices will be without anchor.

This concept of exchange rates is not incompatible with a basically monetary approach, but it gives it another interpretation or, in other words, predicts much more variable quantitative relationships: changes in money may signal a much wider range of financial opportunities instead of a mere change in commodity flow prices at some future time, and changes in national income will, above all, change many asset prices, and in different ways.

Finally, it should be noted that seeing exchange rates as 'double asset prices' entails a typical capital-theoretic view, which has intrigued the Austrians since Menger, Boehm-Bawerk and Hayek.

Diocletian's *pretium verum*

As economists we are so accustomed to the self-evident validity of basic economic concepts that, in most cases, we can no longer perceive their very partial explanatory power. Having been trained, like all the members of the original Austrian School, as an historically oriented lawyer – or rather a jurist – I, personally, have never ceased to wonder at what economists habitually tend to assume. Perhaps most fundamental to economics is the notion of the classical as well as the neoclassical determinate equilibrium price theory, a notion just as basic, if not more so, to critics of the orthodoxy of their day, like Marx or Sraffa, as to 'mainstream' authors. Today this determinate equilibrium price theory is enshrined in General Equilibrium Theory. Do not misunderstand me: I do not doubt the very great usefulness of this standard price theory. On the contrary, I love it. But basically it is the theory of current production and/or current consumption or, in other words, of flow commodities. Alfred Marshall, perhaps its most fervent, though implicit, adherent, gave it its motto: *Natura non facit saltum*[4] – a sentence written in the same second half of the seventeenth and the eighteenth century[5] which gave birth to modern economics. *Natura non facit saltum*: 'in the realm of economics'. I take this to mean that determinate equilibrium prices rest on the foundations of scarcity in production, which are imposed by nature, and on the techniques of production, which are derived from the laws of nature; that consumption rests on preferences which stem from the nature of man; that exchange of commodities is also part of the nature of man;[6] and that, in all this, there is a certain basic continuity, including a continuity of the distribution of income and wealth. Thus, there is not even a single jump in the 'natural' conditions of prices. Now, these notions make for an admirable price theory for pins and potatoes, and even for computers or cellular telephones. They even provide a valid price theory for some assets; but not for the prices of that important class of today's assets whose price the exchange rates express. Exchange rates today are not the (relative) prices of pins or potatoes and not even of computers or cellular telephones.

In order fully to understand a basic economic concept, and that is to say also to understand its limitations, it is good to go back to its historical roots. And the roots of Classical and Neoclassical or, using more modern terminology, of General Equilibrium Price Theory, are not even to be found in the works of Petty or Cantillon, of Adam Smith or Ricardo; they go back much further and are more deeply embedded in fundamental notions of Occidental thought. I would rather not delve into finding out when they really appeared for the first time. But they were first fully manifest, and have been embodied in a full continuity of thought thereafter, in a rescript of the Roman emperors Diocletianus and Maximinianus around AD 300. This rescript has been preserved in and transmitted by the *Codex Iustinianus*, that well-known compendium of Roman Law. And there is manifest proof of the historical continuity from the idea of these two co-emperors up to the present to be seen in the fact that the central tenet of this rescript is still part of present-day Austrian law,[7] no less than of many other codifications of civil law, for example, the Swiss or the French. The *Codex Iustinianus* says in IV, 44, 2 (my stress added):

> Impp. Diocletianus et Maximinianus AA. Aurelio Lupo. Rem *maioris pretii* si tu vel pater tuus *minoris pretii* distraxit, humanum est, ut vel pretium te restituente emptoribus *fundum venditum* recipias auctoritate intercedente iudicis, vel, si emptor elegerit, quod deest *iusto pretio* recipies. minus autem pretium esse videtur, si nec *dimidia pars veri pretii* soluta sit.

To give its main economic gist in translation, this rescript says:

> If a commodity – in particular a piece of land – of a higher value has been bought from you (or your father!) at a lower price it has to be returned to you or, instead, what is missing on the *just price* has to be paid to you. And a price is taken to be too low if *not even half of the true price has been paid*.

Notice first that the notion of a just price which is defined as the true price, and is binding in contracts, was newly introduced into Roman Law at the time of Diocletian: Classical Roman Law was characterized by the principle *caveat emptor*: let the buyer beware.[8] Purchase and sale – one has to distinguish between the two in Roman Law: they were distinct as *emptio* and *venditio* – purchase and sale were consensual contracts and a price, any price determined by free agreement, was before that valid in law. By Diocletian, the freedom of disposition is limited to agreements not too far away from the 'true price', which is the 'just price'.

Note, furthermore, that Diocletian (and his co-emperor) did not assume fraud in their rescript: in case of fraud there were other, and much older, remedies available at law. Their case is different from fraud: possibly the seller (and it is only the seller who is protected by the rescript) does not know the true price and thus lacks information, which is asymmetric. But it is more likely that he is just a seller in a fix, in urgent need of money. The social situation behind the rescript is one of a heavy and increasing tax burden as well as a dwindling population and thus of shrinking markets. In this situation small farms were bought up cheaply by large landholders. The legal literature stresses that the times were also times of inflation.[9] In spite of its factual correctness, however, this argument lacks economic relevance: during inflation the badly informed small seller is likely to be surprised much more by the high price offered by the purchaser. Inflation is a much more valid argument in another sense: the average judge of the time, not yet conversant with inflation, must have been significantly more likely to judge the sales price as too low because, by the time judgement was passed, the money price of land had already risen. So the remedy was likely to impose a very strict limit on legitimate negotiation.

Note, finally, that the emperors Diocletian and Maximinianus were not yet Christians. Thus, the idea of the unique price as the just price predates the predominance of Christianity in the ancient world. Note also that the Bible, both in the Old and the New Testament, does know the notions of *true measure* and *good quality* in economic transactions[10] and implicitly also of a just price; but the just price is not the 'true' price. If anything, the biblical notion of a just price is economically closest to perfect third degree price discrimination: the poor producer should receive more than the rich; and the poor purchaser pay less than the rich. This idea is still embodied in the monastic rule of St Benedict: monks should sell their products at a moderate price in order not to appear avaricious. In other words, the biblical just price is to be determined individually. It is exactly not one which is common to all.

Thus, the idea of Diocletian, or his advisors, was revolutionary and new: even in spite of economic and social upheaval, even in spite of inflation, there is an invariable and unique 'true' price, in particular of land! This price is so well defined that it can be easily found by the judge who has to set it for the would-be buyer, who can either take it or return his purchase. This is *natura non facit saltum* at its starkest, not to say its most implausible. We shall see that exactly for an asset like land, the assumption of a determinate 'true' price is wrong under present circumstances; though it was correct from the fifteenth century up to well into the nineteenth century, when land commonly sold at well-known multiples of its yearly rental value.[11]

Of course, such a well-known social norm shaping common expectations provides an anchor for the notion of a customary price. Adam Smith states:

> The ordinary market price of land, it is to be observed, depends every where upon the ordinary market rate of interest.... When interest was at ten per cent, land was commonly sold for ten or twelve years purchase. As interest sank to six, five, and four per cent, the price of land rose to twenty, five and twenty, and thirty years purchase.... In England it commonly sells at thirty; in France at twenty years purchase.[12]

Historical research has proved him broadly right.[13] Over long time-spans, real estate prices were not constant, but moving slowly according to well-known principles. Such an 'anchor' for asset prices, however, is not founded in technology, individualist preferences or other factor prices, but much rather in social conventions, social mores and commonly held, popular economic 'theories', the latter sometimes being due to the influence of important economists. In changeable times such conventions can break down, leaving nothing in their place.[14]

The Austrian civil law code of 1811, still valid, which, like many other continental law codes, embodies the essence of this rescript of Diocletian, does not speak of a 'true' price but much rather of a '*common*' price. (It also shows, in its nearly identical wording, the influence of Adam Smith's *Wealth of Nations*.)[15]

Actually, the 'common' price is something different again. We have to distinguish, first, the prescientific notion of a 'just' price which, as part of the ground swell of value judgements at the back of people's minds, gave 'fundamental' economic notions their punch. Second, the 'true' price, which, as a determinate long-run equilibrium price, is more or less invariant over time or, at most, slowly moving. It is a 'fundamentally' determined price with even its movement over time being 'fundamentally' determined: for example, the former multiples of yearly rentals constituting the 'true' price of land (in the period when such a thing did exist) moved, as was remarked by many early economists, with the common rate of interest. Third, there is the 'common' price which is the (short-run) market equilibrium price in a competitive market at any moment in time; or, maybe, instead a politically fixed and as such strictly observed price. Even such common prices need not exist, of course, when there are only more or less unconnected transactions of isolated individuals.

The international financial markets, with which we shall be concerned here, in particular the exchange market, are among the most nearly competitive in the world. In these lectures I shall argue, however, that they do have a 'common' price in the sense of a short-run equilibrium market price. But they do not have a 'true' price in the sense of a stable, long-run equilibrium price. A mere supply and demand theory with nothing behind it but the whim of suppliers and demanders is much more general than the price theory of 'fundamentals'. Supply and demand theory as such is therefore not at issue. What is at issue for the assets we shall consider is whether supply and demand curves can be derived respectively from marginal costs and from individual preferences and whether these can be thought of as stable over time. Or, to put it simply, the question is whether in price formation there is any *natura*, any fundamental price determination, outside of human expectations.

Economists might prefer to see these statements presented in the language of economics rather than legal terminology – though, as I intend to show, economic terminology is actually derived from the language of law. So let us turn to an important jurist who is better known as one of the founding fathers of economics. Let us turn to Adam Smith: 'The natural price . . . is, as it were, the central price, to which the prices of all commodities are continually gravitating.'[16] The 'common' price of legal terminology is what Adam Smith calls the market price. It is the short-run price, and not derived by him from any 'fundamentals'. That is quite right. Diocletian's 'true' and therefore 'just' price is Smith's 'natural' price. (In his wording one might detect a harking back to moral overtones: to the possibility that the natural price, being so 'natural', is also the just price.) My question as to the asset markets is: may one assume the existence of such a 'natural' price, 'to which the prices of all commodities are continually gravitating'?

It is my contention that the moral philosopher and teacher of jurisprudence Adam Smith took his notion of the 'natural' price from the old Occidental tradition of the existence of a 'true' price in the sense of the rescript of Diocletian. To my surprise I found, however, that Smith actually *reshaped the notion* of a true price in a very original way; and it is exactly this renovation of the notion of a 'true' price by Adam Smith which became part of the lore of economic thought.

If you read what Richard Cantillon, the first great price theoretician of economics, said about the 'true' price, which he called the 'intrinsic' price and which he, too, contrasted with the market price, you will find that with him it is not, as with Smith, above all an intertemporal price, but much rather an, as it were, interlocal, but simultaneous price. The 'intrinsic' price is the average price of the many different transactions which evidently, and even with Cantillon explicitly, do not all rest on full information and also differ because of varying transaction costs.[17] His notion is very close to the idea of a stable price distribution in the sense of George Stigler's famous search price theory.[18] You find the same notion in Turgot and, in a sense, even more explicitly, in Sir James Steuart: with Steuart, prices diverge from the competitive price, more precisely from the competitive price with double competition, i.e. competition on the side both of suppliers and of demanders. They diverge because in many cases the market is not fully doubly competitive.[19] Thus, before Smith, the 'true' price is the average price – or, in some cases, perhaps the lowest price – a price reckoned over many more or less disconnected transactions in a not perfectly organized market. Evidently that is an important notion of great empirical relevance. But it is not true in the full sense of the rescript of Diocletian (basic for Occidental price-theoretic notions) where prices are not allowed to diverge too much over time from their 'true' level. Up to Smith, the 'intrinsic' price of Cantillon, and similar notions of other authors, are thus, to use probabilistic terminology or the terminology of financial markets, statements about an average value or, perhaps, a lowest expected value, but they are not statements about the volatility of price or its intertemporal variance. This they become only with Adam Smith and ever more thereafter. His statement is one of temporal price convergence:

The 'natural' price is the one 'to which prices of all commodities are *continually gravitating*'. It is remarkable that this notion became explicit only with Smith; for Cantillon or Turgot used basically the same analysis of fundamentals as Smith, but did not draw his intertemporal conclusion. It is the particular notion, new to economics, of Smith which we shall need for the analysis of assets and in particular the assets in financial markets and, even more particularly, for exchange rates. These are traded on highly organized markets so that the question of differences in information or transaction costs as reasons for different prices at the same time does not arise. Our question will be: is there, with them, a fundamentally determined price towards which each one of them is 'continually gravitating'? And was the ghost of Diocletian still around, even in his quantitative precision, when Fischer Black (a Nobel Prize candidate, unfortunately dying prematurely) laid it down that 'we might define an efficient market as one in which price is within a factor of 2 of value'?[20]

It is still to be shown that a continuous thread of thought runs from Diocletian's notion of the 'true' and also 'just' price to Adam Smith's 'natural' price and further to standard economic price theory stemming from him.

The scholastic renaissance of the High Middle Ages (eleventh to twelfth century) was a renaissance of Roman Law no less than of the philosophy of the later centuries of ancient Europe. Southern has pointed out how the archcanonist Gratian brought about a junction of Roman Law and canon law, the law of the Church,[21] which in the Dark Ages had already been said to live according to Roman Law. In particular, the moral theory for commercial life was largely taken from Roman Law. In the later Middle Ages and the Early Modern period the case discussed and regulated in Diocletian's rescript was called a *laesio enormis*.[22] Buying for less than half the 'true price' meant hurting one's partner to the contract enormously, even, as the word implies, hurting him physically; and up to the present day, every Austrian lawyer would learn this trope under the very name of *laesio enormis*. Price-theoretic thought along these lines was characteristic of the later School Men, of St Bernardin of Siena in the fifteenth century and of the School of Salamanca in the sixteenth century.[23] And it is well known that, on the question of commercial morals, Martin Luther did not deviate at all from standard Catholic doctrine. Actually, the early modern period, a period both of great social upheavals and of an (inflationary) 'price revolution', was the heyday of discussion and reinvigoration of Diocletian's price-theoretic notions.

Coming closer to the dawn of modern economics, it has to be remembered that both the Dutch Republic and also Scotland – in contrast to England – were countries strictly adhering to the revived Roman Law. Among early economists, Petty was taught by the Jesuits in France. John Locke was a learned 'civil' lawyer, i.e. trained in the Roman Law applicable in Church courts, even in England. Richard Cantillon was a Roman

Catholic and cites the fine canon law distinctions of *lucrum cessans* and *damnum emergens* in his discussion of interest. In his price theory the telltale price margins of one half and of double the price of the *laesio enormis* are explicitly mentioned.[24] Adam Smith was well-versed in 'natural law' ideas which stemmed partly from Roman Law traditions. Smith was a theoretician of law in a Roman Law country, Scotland. It is quite clear then that many of the early economists were close to the original Roman Law concept of the existence of a well-defined and determinate 'true' price as a 'fundamental' price, and a price of which we might think as a long-term 'central' price. The idea of the existence of a 'true', 'natural', 'central' and 'fundamental' price is hoary with age, so that it is quite 'natural' not to question it. But this does not necessarily make such prescientific notions more true, and certainly not necessarily true in all cases.

Price-theoretic fundamentals of modern economics and their inapplicability to certain assets

In modern economics it is by now an elementary exercise to derive price-theoretic 'fundamentals'. For the case of international financial markets in general and exchange rates in particular we can happily leave aside all the thorny problems which arise outside of perfectly competitive markets. For, financial markets and, in particular, those of exchange rates of the great currencies are among the markets which are generally agreed to be closest in reality to the ideal theoretical case of perfect competition. So we can stick to competitive analysis.

In the case of perfect competition we know that for goods of current consumption demand curves are nothing but the expression of the preferences of the relevant consumers; and supply curves an aggregation of the marginal costs of suppliers. For intermediate goods, the case is already a little more difficult. Here the demand curve is derived at one remove from the preferences of the ultimate consumers, but in a well understood way. Thus, in these cases of currently produced and currently supplied commodities, we have 'fundamentally' determined supplies and demands, and it is plausible that in a free and well-organized market a price equilibrium should be reached easily.

Difficulties already start to arise in the case of durable capital goods; and business cycle literature attests to these difficulties. Even so, in the case of durable capital goods, we still have a 'fundamental' supply price which we may call the cost of reproduction of this capital good. It is determined by the marginal cost of finally producing it. Reproduction might, of course, have to pass through a complicated series of temporal steps. But still, this cost of reproduction is, in general, well definable. There is also, on principle, a well-defined demand price, which we may call the production price of the capital good. This is the series of all the periodical marginal products to be derived from it during its future life, each future marginal product discounted by a suitably chosen rate of interest up to the present, and then summed over all periods. Note that here a price-theoretic equilibrium is already much more in doubt: for if demand changes it may take a considerable period of time until new capital goods come to market in sufficient quantities, so that the price deviates from long-run equilibrium for some considerable period. Every student knows that, in fact, stability of this long-run equilibrium is not absolutely assured either, i.e. it is no longer certain that there is a 'natural' price in the sense of Smith, which by its definition as a continual centre of gravity pre-supposes stability of the adjustment process. Furthermore, techniques may already have changed, though this may not yet be evident to everyone. What the production cost will actually be thus becomes a question to be judged individually. Nor is it clear what demand conditions will be like in the future; how long the useful life of the capital good in question may last; and, above all, with what rate of interest to discount returns to the present. To put it a little differently: future demand is uncertain, as Menger[25] had stressed, and perhaps even more subjective is actual cost, as Hayek[26] never tired of pointing out. Fundamentals do still exist for durable capital goods, but they are hidden in a more or less thick fog of subjective judgement and may be revealed to participants only at some future point of time.

All these difficulties are magnified in the case of the assets of potentially infinite durability with which we are concerned in these lectures: with gold and precious metals, with common stock, with real estate, with the art of Old (and already dead) Masters, and with internationally traded moneys, the relative prices of which are the exchange rates. In all of these cases there is no relevant production cost: the basic supply-side fundamental drops out.

Pictures by Old Masters were once produced at some cost. But by now this cost has become irrelevant because the Master in question is dead and genuine reproduction therefore impossible. The former costs have become irrelevant by now, they are simply sunk costs. Real estate, land as such, is equally non-reproducible. Financial assets, and especially moneys, on the other hand, have no cost price – for another reason: they are reproducible at zero cost, or near zero cost. They represent commodities produced at cost, but they themselves have been created at no cost. And even gold – or, on the other hand, common stock – is of a similar nature: it is currently reproduced, for sure; but the production stream is small relative to the large volume of existing stock,[27] which can be used with little wastage over and over again. The cost of current reproduction is therefore of little importance relative to the stock price. Or, to put the same point in another way: it takes an extremely long time until a given shortage of demand can be supplied from current production; and an excess supply can never be rectified by any changes in quantity. For, the given supply quantity lasts indefinitely. Therefore, all of these assets can at best have a 'fundamentally' determined demand, but no such supply. Though, as we shall see, actually they do not even have a fundamental demand value in the usual sense.

In order to realize that a fundamentally determined demand value is lacking we can best turn to auction theory. Modern auction theory[28] assumes that there is a well defined distribution function of the valuations of potential demanders for the commodities to be auctioned. This distribution function is known to the seller – and possibly also to the demanders. But the seller does not know what the demanders' valuations are with which he is actually faced: these demanders are drawn at random out of the distribution. It is usually assumed that the distribution function of the valuations has finite support, in fact that – for convenience of calculation – it is a rectangular distribution. This is no serious limitation as a wide class of continuous distribution functions can be transformed into rectangular ones.

The problem we are interested in is: what do the valuations in the distribution function underlying auction theory actually mean? Auction theory discusses two possibilities: *private values* and *common values*.

Private values pertain to the personal use of the demander; they are thought of as independent of the valuation of anyone else. They correspond to purely individualist preferences. As was standard in particular in the Austrian theory – derived, in this respect, from nineteenth-century German economic thought – individuals were assumed to be typically *different in their tastes and fortunes*. It is plausible that a certain painting is not valued in the same way by everyone: there are rich connoisseurs who value it highly, and from them valuation gradually decreases downward to those who merely think a picture is good to cover a crack in the wall.

Common values, on the other hand, in their pure form take into account only the supposed valuation of others. The typical case in the literature on auctions is the purchase from government of the right to prospect for oil. If oil should actually be found it would not be employed, let us say, as an ointment for the purchaser's sore toes. No, oil is produced for sale in order to make a profit.[29] Basically, common values are therefore always values for a supposed resale at some future occasion.

It is the purely private-value auction, in particular with risk-neutral bidders, which provides the prototype for standard competitive analysis. In this case, simple mechanisms are at hand, where no strategic behaviour taking account of the actions of others is necessary in order to achieve individually optimal results. A case in question would be the 'English auction' with ascending bids where the commodity auctioned goes to the bidder with the highest valuation – at the value bid by the bidder with the second highest valuation. In a well-known article Wilson showed[30] that in the private value auction under certain regularity conditions the price converges to the competitive price as the number of bidders increases, in spite of the fact that this competitive price is not known to bidders. Here, then, we have a 'true' or 'fundamental' price.

With common values, however, strategic action is always necessary: in this case one has to ask how others estimate the value common to all. The distribution of valuation is commonly explained as the individual judgements of the common value by different bidders, some underestimating, some overestimating it. Here then is the possibility of the 'winner's curse': he who outbids the others is the one who has actually overvalued the commodity in question most and is therefore likely to make the greatest loss in a resale. In order not to suffer from the winner's curse, each bidder therefore has to downgrade his individual bid by a complicated estimation of the distribution of over- and under-valuations of all the bidders; and he has to guess or to learn whether he is a high or a low estimator and possibly even the highest estimator who is probably overpricing to the highest degree. Thus, even if there are cost fundamentals at the back of the bidders' minds, they are clouded by their imperfect information. Costs are estimated with an error; preferences in the usual sense, on the other hand, do not exist in the case of purely common values.

But in the case of common-value auctions, even these costs estimated with error and clouded by strategic behaviour need not exist at all. They do exist in the cases usually analysed: the government auction of oil prospecting rights where the oil, which may eventually be found, has a fundamentally determined value generated by marginal costs and marginal utilities in their aggregate totality; or the auction of wavelengths for cellular telephone systems. But not so in the case of long-lived assets, which can be produced without cost or whose former costs of production are by now sunk costs.

In the case of such assets a common-value auction has, as always, no demand 'fundamental': there are no individual preferences for personal use of the commodity. The whole point of buying is to have an asset which may yield some current return but, above all, has a resale value at some future point in time, as yet undetermined. This point in time might occur when either a better investment alternative arises or when the value of (a part of) one's wealth has to be realized because of some personal need or a change in personal circumstances, for example, death and inheritance by agents with other preferences and other financial circumstances.[31] This, of course, assumes that not all market participants have the same opinion about price and that not all opinions stay constant over time, for otherwise a uniquc and stable market opinion is once more a well-determined 'fundamental';[32] or that individuals differ in risk aversion. In case of an indestructible asset with either only sunk costs in the past or no production costs as such there is thus not only no demand 'fundamental', but no cost fundamental either. The price is without anchor either in preferences or in costs. There is, of course, at any moment an asset demand and an asset supply; there is, as we might say, harking back to legal terminology, a 'common' price, the market price of the moment. But there is no 'true', i.e. fundamental price. And therefore there does not exist a 'natural' price in the sense of Smith, a price towards which the market price over time should 'continually gravitate'.

Keynes put it nicely in his beauty contest simile: price is nothing but 'what average opinion expects the average opinion to be'.[33] Even in this case there may be 'fundamentals': general opinion may have a traditionally determined notion of what such an asset price should be, as was the case with respect to real estate for centuries. But in an age of constant innovation that is unlikely. For the analysis of innovation we have to turn to Schumpeter and also to Hayek. But before we do so, we first have to take a look at General Equilibrium Price Theory.

It is well known that the basic model of competitive General Equilibrium Analysis[34] deals with a futureless world of certainty. But also that the uncertainties of the future – or rather of situations of risk evolving in the future – have been incorporated into this analysis by the ingenious device of contingent contracts, contingent upon some definable state of nature in the future. The idealized financial instrument in which one could insure oneself against any future chance occurrence is called an 'Arrow-Debreu-Security'. In the case of complete financial markets in such Arrow-Debreu-Securities for all conceivable chance occurrences at later points of time, the uncertainties of the future are once more traded away.

But, of course, in the cases of long-lived, not currently or only to a very small extent currently produced (or produced without cost) goods, i.e. of internationally traded assets, we are bound to remain in a state of incomplete markets; and in this we are not likely to be helped even by Roy Radner's ingenious method to get around the problem.[35] Radner postulated a spanning condition, where non-existent financial assets can be substituted by other, existing ones. Perhaps the least important point is that General Equilibrium Analysis always has to postulate a finite world, while the typical internationally traded asset has a potentially infinite life span. It is much more important that the vast possible number of relevant future chance occurrences makes it impossible even simply to define all relevant states of nature, let alone estimate the probabilities of their occurrences; that approximately 'complete' contracts are likely to become prohibitively costly to formulate; and that dealing with the myriad of possible circumstances in the distant future is bound to make markets, if they should exist at all, very thin, so that they would no longer be competitive. Probably the best and simplest argument against the completeness of financial markets is a practical and realistic one: even for the most common exchange rates, futures markets for the more distant future simply do not exist. So the appeal to General Equilibrium Analysis, this most 'fundamental' of all fundamental analyses, lands us once more in the dilemma that in the case of internationally traded financial assets it is most likely that there is nothing apart from the average opinion of what average opinion is.

In recent years General Equilibrium Analysis itself has turned more and more to situations of incomplete markets. In the *Festschrift* for

Debreu, Torsten Hens[36] summarized work by MasCollel and Magill and Quinzii:[37] for the case of nominally denominated financial assets, which are so important in international financial markets, he showed that there will be a multiplicity of equilibria which depend upon the amount of money in circulation. Thus, it is precisely General Equilibrium Analysis that leaves us with nothing but the indeterminacy of price and a non-neutrality of money – which runs counter to 'real' fundamentals.

The purpose of this long exercise was to show that economists instinctively search for a 'true' price for everything and a 'natural' price towards which prices tend to converge; but they are not aware that, in this, they are following a long tradition of legal theory and moral philosophy. There are no fundamentals, however, in the sense of individual preferences or technically determined supply conditions: first in so far as (more or less) eternally-lived assets are concerned, which have only sunk costs or no costs of reproduction at all, or are reproduced in a mere trickle relative to existing stock; and second in so far as such assets are concerned which, to a large extent, are being bought for potential resale at an unknown future point in time. But exactly those two aspects characterize the kinds of assets traded in international financial markets and, in particular, in foreign exchanges. At any moment their price depends only upon the average opinion of what average opinion is and will be in the future. This average opinion may itself depend at one remove on some kind of imagined 'fundamental'. But that is likely to be so only in traditional societies where long-lived assets have conventional values. In a society of constant innovation this is unlikely. The prices of these kinds of assets – Old Masters, real estate, bonds, even common stock and especially internationally traded moneys, i.e. foreign exchanges – will typically be without an anchor. We should not be surprised at all if their prices do not conform to any fundamentals. Rather, it is the other way around: it should come as a surprise if occasionally, during very calm periods, they do conform to clear-cut 'fundamentals'.

Schumpeter, Hayek and Keynes on innovation and entrepreneurship

It may very well be the most astonishing feature of Joseph A. Schumpeter's *Theory of Economic Development* that his central figure, the entrepreneur, who causes creative destruction and brings about new combinations, is not guided by a theory of a 'true' and 'natural' price. In fact, Schumpeter stresses that his entrepreneur lacks sufficient data to evaluate the 'fundamentals' of his new enterprise. He is only guided by intuition.[38] And in a sense this is close to being obvious: whence should the innovative entrepreneur derive the demand function for his product, which as yet has not been marketed? And as innovation frequently entails uncertain development costs which are sunk costs before full-scale production is even started, it is extremely difficult to judge costs in advance. Thus the entrepreneur is faced with an incalculable, genuine uncertainty. In the spirit of Schumpeter, our question will therefore be: are the prices of international financial assets, and above all of foreign exchanges, not such incalculable prices due to constant innovation? Does not the financial literature constantly use Schumpeter's term 'innovations' to denote the stream of new information? And should this term not be taken seriously in the sense in which Schumpeter used it?

Perhaps even more surprising is Schumpeter's idea that innovations are financed by bank credit and that the rate of interest arises only in a dynamic context characterized by entrepreneurial innovations.

It is not implausible that the creative entrepreneur should find it difficult to calculate the risks of his endeavour at all accurately. But a bank extending credit to him? It is certainly one of the looser strands of Schumpeter's theory that he assumes that just any banker is likely to extend credit to the proponent of an incalculable venture.[39] Actually, we watch bankers taking incredible risks all the time in international financial markets and, of course, frequently getting seriously bitten. Just think of the relatively recent instance of ten of the world's largest banks making breathtaking losses in the wake of the debacle of Long-Term Capital Management.[40] Evidently, hard-bitten bankers are no less prone to fall victim to seemingly plausible schemes than other gullible financiers. To make Schumpeter's notion a little less strange we may take it that banks assume a calculated probability distribution of failures and charge a much higher than normal rate of interest when financing (without sufficient collateral) risky and innovative ventures, or that they eventually become, at least to some extent, equity holders of the 'creative' entrepreneurs.

Strangest of all is Schumpeter's idea that the rate of interest as such is only due to innovation and thus to deviations from the static framework.[41] At that, any Ricardian, Sraffian, von Neumannian (if there is such a person) will rise up in arms; and actually Schumpeter was immediately taken to task for this unforgivable heresy by the then guardian of economic orthodoxy in Austria, the President of the Austrian Academy of Sciences, Eugen Ritter Boehm von Bawerk.[42] I would rather not fall under a like anathema. But at least we may appropriate Schumpeter's notion that the level of the real rate of interest depends upon the volume of innovation and the amount of disequilibrium profits, as well as on more conventional aspects of production. Furthermore, it should be obvious at least that the realized rate of return on capital in an economy will be the higher, the fewer serious bankruptcies there are. For the question at hand there is an important conclusion to be drawn: the real rate of interest in an economy may also depend upon the profits to be made in international financial markets and thus also on the exchange rates. Money and monetary forces may be non-neutral with respect to the real rate of interest and may be so for a very long period of time.

Hayek's price-theoretic ideas are frequently cited as an important source of the concept of efficient markets for financial instruments. In spite of the substantial conceptional and ideological differences between Hayek and Schumpeter, the price theory of the mature Hayek is actually very similar to that of the young Schumpeter; only, with Hayek, every economic agent is – in price-theoretic terms – an entrepreneur in the sense of Schumpeter: all costs of capital goods are subjective because of the difficulty of judging future demand constellations, of judging obsolescence correctly and of knowing the technical developments in advance which will shape future reproduction costs. Furthermore, all production techniques are only subjectively known and cannot be fully communicated to others, because individuals do not even know what implicit and subconsciously known knowledge they utilize.[43] All these very subjective informations are constantly changing, so that innovation is, on the one hand, usually minute and, on the other, continuously occurring. (This is in contrast to Schumpeter, who thought innovation to be one of various basically large jumps which occur discontinuously.)

Hayek needed these price-theoretic ideas to argue against the possibility of socialist planning, which would be possible in principle if price-theoretic fundamentals were clearly known to the planning authorities and not changing too quickly. For our purpose of international financial markets we can learn from Hayek that participants in the markets can, at best, be thought of as engaged in constant error correction behaviour groping towards ever changing fundamentals clouded in a thick fog of ignorance.

Such a groping requires constant 'alertness' on the side of market participants. Such alertness for opportunities is the central characteristic which, according to Israel Kirzner, marks the entrepreneur as such.[44]

What the Austrians, be they Schumpeter or Hayek, did not think out sufficiently is the dependence of economic decisions on notions of *what other agents think*. Being basically individualistic, the Austrians instinctively thought in private-value terms and not in common-value terms in the sense of auction theory. As I see it, assets in financial markets are, however, basically held for resale at an uncertain future point in time. Some ideas about such an interdependence of decision taking in financial markets can be found in Keynes' *General Theory*.

According to Keynes, it is the rate of interest which is particularly sensitive to changing moods,[45] a fact already noted by Cantillon. Nowadays, however, it is much rather the exchange rate which is so conditioned. A key notion of Keynes which we have to remember is his dictum: it is interesting to what degree 'the stability of the system and its sensitiveness to changes . . . should be so dependent on the existence of a *variety* of opinion about what is uncertain'.[46] Shifts in the dispersion of opinion about the 'market' are indeed of great importance in explaining shifts in the volatility of prices.

Notes

1 Ronald MacDonald, 'Exchange Rate Behaviour: Are Fundamentals Important?', *Economic Journal*, 109 (1999a), F673–F691, here p. F673.
2 Huw Dixon, 'Controversy: Exchange Rates and Fundamentals', *Economic Journal*, 109 (1999), F652–F654, here p. F652.
3 Milton Friedman, 'The Quantity Theory of Money: A Restatement', in: M. Friedman (ed.), *Studies in the Quantity Theory of Money*, Chicago 1956, pp. 3–21, here p. 4.
4 Alfred Marshall, *Principles of Economics*, London, 1st edn, 1890, motto on the title page.
5 The sentence *natura non facit saltus* (plural) was coined in his *Nouveaux essais*, 1701–1704, by G.W. Leibniz (against J. Locke) and used by C. von Linné (1751).
6 See Adam Smith, *An Inquiry into the Nature and Causes of the Wealth of Nations*, London 1776, 'Glasgow Edition', Oxford 1976, I.ii, especially 2.
7 See the *Austrian Civil Law Code* (AbGB, §934 and §935).
8 See, e.g. Max Kaser, *Römisches Privatrecht*, 3rd edn, Munich–Berlin 1964, p. 161.
9 Ibid.
10 *Lev*. 16, 36; *Dtn*. 25, 15f., etc.
11 For the English Middle Ages with land prices reckoned at about 10 to 14 times the rental value, see Sylvia L. Thrupp, *The Merchant Class of Medieval London* [1300–1500], Ann Arbor 1962, p. 122f.
12 Smith (1776), II.iv.17.
13 See especially Hrothgar John Habakkuk, 'The Long-Term Rate of Interest and the Price of Land in the Seventeenth Century', *Economic History Review*, II.5 (1952), 26–45; the same, 'The Price of Land in England 1500–1700', in: W. Abel *et al.* (eds), *Wirtschaft, Geschichte und Wirtschaftsgeschichte, Festschrift zum 65. Geburtstag von Friedrich Lütge*, Stuttgart 1966, pp. 119–28.
14 Diocletian's edict was geared in particular towards the highly sensitive price of real estate in a mainly agrarian society. But that – outside of a traditional society and contrary to age-old popular lore – there is not even 'security' in real estate values can best be shown by recent Japanese commercial property prices. See *The Economist*, vol. 356, no. 8181, 29 July 2000, p. 78: 'Since 1990, the value of Japanese property has plunged by over 60 percent. In Tokyo, commercial property has shed more than three quarters of its value.'
15 ABGB §934 (see note 7).
16 Smith (1776), I.vii.15.
17 Richard Cantillon, *Essai sur la Nature du Commerce en Général*, 'Londres' 1755 (originally English, around 1730), part I, ch. 10 and part II, ch. 2.
18 George J. Stigler, 'The Economics of Information', *Journal of Political Economy*, 69 (1961), 213–25.
19 Sir James Steuart, *An Inquiry into the Principles of Political Oeconomy*, London 1767, Book II, ch. 7.
20 Fischer Black, 'Noise', *Journal of Finance*, 41 (1986), 529–43, here p. 533.
21 Richard Southern, *Scholastic Humanism and the Unification of Europe*, vol. I, Oxford 1995; see especially 'V. Gratian's Change of Mind about Roman Law', pp. 295ff. and 'VIII. The First Masterpiece of Scholastic Humanism', pp. 305ff.
22 See Kaser, quoted in note 8.
23 See Henry W. Spiegel, *The Growth of Economic Thought*, Englewood Cliffs, NJ 1971, pp. 60f., 88f., 679.
24 Cantillon, op. cit., part II, ch. 9. 'One half' and 'double' the price are given as price margins in part I, ch. 10.

25 Carl Menger, *Principles of Economics* (J. Dingwall and B.F. Hoselitz, trans. and eds), Glencoe, IL 1950 (originally in German 1871), ch. 1, part 4, pp. 67ff.
26 See, e.g. Friedrich A. Hayek, *Collectivist Economic Planning*, London 1935, pp. 167ff.; Friedrich A. Hayek, 'Socialist Calculation: The Competitive Solution', *Economica*, N.S. 7 (1940), 125–49, here p. 140f.
27 Similar to this argument, Franklin Allen and Douglas Gale, 'Bubbles and Crises', *Economic Journal*, 110 (2000), 236–55, have shown in a setting with risk shifting (bank credit with the banks having to shoulder the loss of bankruptcies) that risky assets in fixed supply are liable to show non-fundamental 'bubble' pricing.
28 See, e.g. the survey article by R. Preston McAfee and John McMillan, 'Auctions and Bidding', *Journal of Economic Literature*, 25 (1987), 699–738.
29 Recently auctions of airwaves have been frequent. See, e.g. R. Preston McAfee and John McMillan, 'Analyzing the Airwaves Auction', *Journal of Economic Perspectives*, 10 (1996), 159–77. The financial press has been paying quite a bit of attention to the highly successful mobile phone licence auction in Britain in early 2000.
30 Robert Wilson, 'A Bidding Model of Perfect Competition', *Review of Economic Studies*, 59 (1977), 171–8.
31 Exactly for such unforeseen liquidity needs and for the case of limited market participation due to a fixed cost of entering a given market, Franklin Allen and Douglas Gale, 'Limited Market Participation and Volatility of Asset Prices', *American Economic Review*, 84 (1994), 933–55, have demonstrated deviation of asset prices from their 'fundamentals'.
32 See, e.g. the models of Lawrence R. Glosten and Paul R. Milgrom, 'Bid, Ask, and Transaction Prices in a Specialist Market with Heterogeneously Informed Traders', *Journal of Financial Economics*, 14 (1985), 71–100; or Franklin Allen and Douglas Gale, 'Limited Market Participation and Volatility of Asset Prices', *American Economic Review*, 84 (1994), 933–55.
33 John M. Keynes, *The General Theory of Employment Interest and Money*, London 1936, ch. 12, p. 156.
34 See, e.g. Kenneth J. Arrow and Frank Hahn, *General Competitive Analysis*, San Francisco and Edinburgh 1971.
35 Roy Radner, 'Competitive Equilibrium under Uncertainty', *Econometrica*, 36 (1968), pp. 31–58.
36 Thorsten Hens, 'Incomplete Markets', in: A. Kirman (ed.), *Elements of General Equilibrium Analysis* (dedicated to Gerard Debreu), Oxford 1998, ch. 5, pp. 139–210.
37 Michael J.P. Magill and Martine Quinzii, 'Real Effects of Money in General Equilibrium', *Journal of Mathematical Economics*, 21 (1992), 301–42; the same, 'Incomplete Markets over an Infinite Horizon: Long-Lived Securities and Speculative Bubbles', *Journal of Mathematical Economics*, 26 (1996), 133–70.
38 Joseph A. Schumpeter, *The Theory of Economic Development* (R. Opie trans., originally in German 1912), Cambridge, MA 1934, reprint New York 1961, pp. 84ff:

> Outside of these accustomed channels the individual is without those data for his decisions and those rules of conduct which are usually very accurately known to him within them.... Many things must remain uncertain, still others are only ascertainable within wide limits, some can perhaps only be 'guessed'.... Here the success of everything depends upon intuition, the capacity of seeing things in a way which afterwards proves to be true.

39 Ibid., basically in the whole of chapter III, 'Credit and Capital', pp. 95ff. Banks are defined as businesses for granting credit (p. 98), and 'in principle no one other than the entrepreneur needs credit' (p. 102).

40 See Franklin R. Edwards, 'Hedge Funds and the Collapse of Long-Term Capital Management', *Journal of Economic Perspectives*, 13 (1999), 1pp. 189–210.

41 Schumpeter, op. cit., ch. V, 'Interest on Capital', pp. 157ff. P. 175 summarizes: 'Interest . . . is a product of development'.

42 Eugen Ritter Boehm von Bawerk, 'Eine "dynamische" Theorie des Kapitalzinses', *Zeitschrift für Volkswirtschaft, Sozialpolitik und Verwaltung*, 22 (1913), 1–62.

43 Friedrich A. Hayek, 'The Use of Knowledge in Society', *American Economic Review*, 35 (1945), 517–30; see also note 25.

44 Israel M. Kirzner, *Competition and Entrepreneurship*, Chicago 1973.

45 Keynes op. cit., ch. 13, ch. 15.

46 Keynes op. cit., ch. 13, p. 172.

Lecture II Preliminaries

Friedman's case for flexible exchange rates versus random walks in theory and practice

Stabilizing expectations?

In what turned out to be arguably his most influential economic tract, *The Case for Flexible Exchange Rates*, Milton Friedman pronounced already in 1950 that 'a system of flexible or floating exchange rates [is] . . . absolutely essential for the fulfilment of our basic economic objective: the achievement and maintenance of a free and prosperous world community engaging in unrestricted multilateral trade.' He expressed the opinion that 'liberalization of trade,. . . harmonization of internal monetary and fiscal policies' and, be it noted in first place, 'promotion of rearmament' (no anti-armament man he, in contrast to Adam Smith) 'become far easier to solve in a world of flexible exchange rates and its corollary, free convertibility of currencies'.[1]

This founding credo of what one might call the present Anglo-American orthodoxy as to the indubitable merits of flexible exchange rates is faulty in many respects – faulty both historically and in terms of political economy and, above all, in its price-theoretic foundations.

It is faulty first of all historically, as the classical gold standard of the last quarter of the nineteenth century, if not already earlier, and up to 1914 was certainly the very heyday of the liberalization of trade. Probably, one could call the period of the classical gold standard a period of 'harmonization of internal monetary and fiscal policies', apart from the fact that it is not easy to define what is really meant by the term 'harmonization'. And the classical gold standard certainly did not at all impede the 'promotion of rearmament'. Rapid rearmament, as Boehm von Bawerk pointed out[2] – in what was the first theoretical statement of the doctrine of 'twin deficits' – led to rapid foreign indebtedness. But it was exactly one of the merits of the gold standard that, in case of need, a government could very easily go into debt – into *international* debt. In fact, this was the reason why latecomers to the gold standard adopted it in the first place, the Austro-Hungarian Monarchy being a case in question.

The argument that flexible exchange rates are a 'corollary' of 'free convertibility of currencies' is not only wrong on historical grounds, as the classical gold standard was the very epitome of convertibility. It is also wrong on the grounds of political economy. In terms of political economy the Nobel Laureate Robert Mundell made the well-known point that at any one time you can have only two of the following three good things: fixed exchange rates, free capital mobility (which is the highest form of convertibility of the currency) and an autonomous monetary policy.[3] So you *can* have free capital mobility without a flexible exchange rate, as we Austrians know after having lived very prosperously for eighteen years, from 1981 to 1998, with an exchange rate tightly linked to the German mark; or as, of course, all European countries within the euro now know. Flexible exchange rates are *not* the political 'corollary' of the free convertibility of currencies. But then, of course, you have to give up your autonomy of monetary policy (which I take to be an instance of a very 'harmonious' monetary policy in the sense of Friedman).

Actually, I think even the dictum of Robert Mundell is by now no longer completely correct. In a world of more or less entirely free and very large 'globalized' capital movements, in a world in which transactions on capital account make up something like 98 per cent or more of all foreign exchange transactions, you cannot have autonomy of monetary policy anyway, full stop; at least not unless you are the one country whose currency dominates the foreign exchange markets, and that is still the United States of America with its dollar.

Empirical proof of this is that the long-run real interest rate of the Deutsche Mark depended upon the dollar–mark exchange rate;[4] or, to put the point differently, that all central banks other than the Federal Reserve have to take their country's exchange rate into account when setting their monetary policy.[5] What the choice of the exchange rate entails is merely that, with a flexible rate, you need somewhat smaller international reserves than with a fixed one; which need not be an expensive choice because you can earn very substantial interest returns if you manage your reserves well.

But these flaws in Friedman's plea for flexible exchange rates pale beside his fundamental error in price theory. Friedman did not realize that in the case of 'free convertibility of currencies', as he put it, or with free capital mobility of a very substantial amount of international capital, as I would put it, you need an *asset approach* to exchange rate pricing. And in this case you need a price theory that recognizes that there are no 'fundamentals' to exchange rates. As is well known, Friedman was a great admirer of Alfred Marshall in his early years and taught a course in price theory along strictly Marshallian lines. And Marshall is the prophet of *natura non facit saltum* in economics. Or, to put it in a nutshell, Friedman is a classic proponent of the price theory of the Emperor Diocletian and tried to apply it to exchange rate theory.

It would be incorrect to say that Friedman's so highly influential tract does not mention capital movements in foreign exchange markets. But, basically, his capital movements are only those which another Nobel Laureate, Sir James Meade, in his famous book, *The Balance of Payments*,[6] called 'accommodating' transactions: They are only the other side to current account imbalances; and as they merely 'accommodate' these imbalances, they do not change prices. In fact, that is more or less the definition of 'accommodation': capital movements which behave in such a way that prices do not have to change. In another instance Friedman speaks of 'capital' transactions[7] – explicitly in inverted commas – in case of speculative attack. Here these capital movements probably *do* change prices, but implicitly only temporarily. The 'natural' price of exchange rates in the sense of Adam Smith is not changed and remains to be determined by 'fundamentals', which in their turn are determined by the export and import flows alone. Without ever actually saying so, Milton Friedman implicitly assumes that capital movements do not change the fundamentally determined exchange rate, and thus already assumes a priori what he goes out to prove.

Now, as of the year 1950, Friedman may be excused for this line of thought: at that time, capital flows, particularly shifts in already existing financial assets between countries, were tiny trickles. The tragedy of historical development was that by 1973, when the United States rapidly embraced the change to flexible exchange rates originally forced upon them and embraced it wholeheartedly partly *because* Friedman had convinced so many in the profession of the virtues of flexible exchange rates, this was no longer factually correct: capital movements had already swelled considerably. And by now to ignore capital movements and their much more than temporary effects on exchange rates is, of course, wholly beside the point.

At this stage we have to turn briefly to another misunderstanding closely linked to that of Friedman: international capital movements, it is frequently argued, are not at all large, even in our present world. For capital movements are identical with the current account imbalances. Now, it is true that current account imbalances constitute the flow of newly created (or net quantity of) capital between nations. For the equivalent of, for example, any excess of imports over exports of a country is, of necessity, either the creation of an additional international debt title or an international sale of an asset; unless 'exports' or 'imports' are gifts when, according to national income statistics, they would not even count as exports or imports. But the change of any kind of capital stock is the net quantity flow of capital only if and when the capital price does not change. In general, the percentage change of the value of any stock is (at first approximation, for example for infinitesimally small changes) the percentage change of quantity (for given price) plus the percentage change of price (for given quantity).[8] In this terminology the current account imbalance corresponds only to the quantity change of the capital account of a nation. The price change, on the other hand, has very much to do with the gross capital transactions. More precisely, it depends on differential changes in information, in transaction costs and in risk preferences between traders as well as in changes in preferences, and all this chiefly for already existing ('old') assets, including debt titles. The resulting changes in exchange rates will, of course, also determine even the value of the balance on current account. Therefore, it is a grave mistake to try to determine the value of the exchange rate simply from any independently given export and import decisions of economic agents, disregarding asset pricing considerations, or, in other words, as though asset pricing decisions did not already produce data influencing exports and imports as well.

To give a simple example of this frequently forgotten truism, forgotten basically because the most primitive tenets of capital theory have been ignored: let us assume that the world consists only of the United States and Europe, let us furthermore assume that the balance on current account between the USA and Euro-Europe is zero and stays so, and let us finally assume that the net credit position of US-residents relative to Europe (i.e. net in dollars) is one trillion dollars, while the net debt position of US-residents relative to Europe (i.e. net in euro) is one and a half trillion euro. At an exchange rate of one dollar per euro the USA are then very heavily a debtor nation while, with a shift to an exchange rate of one half a dollar per euro, the USA have suddenly become a substantial creditor nation. All this was a simple consequence of the denomination of debt instruments in terms of different currencies and the concomitant change in asset prices due to a change in exchange rates – perhaps because of a change in preferences between euros and dollars; and all this had nothing to do with any, perhaps sustained, imbalance in the current account, which by assumption remained nonexistent. All this was the consequence of a simple price change. It is not at all true that the sum of the current account and the capital account of each country have to sum to zero if the two have to be measured differently.

With more than two countries, a further possibility arises: 'old' capital assets may be exchanged against each other without a change in the net asset position of the transactor. A Euro-European may, for example, exchange his holding of yen assets against US-dollar assets, which entails a capital movement out of Japan and into the USA, without any change in current accounts and even without necessarily changing capital prices, though an exchange rate change would be likely. In other words: changes in financial investment preferences are most likely to change exchange rates.

And, of course, as far as exchange rates go, any substitution of one kind of money against another asset must be considered a capital transaction. These substitutions make up an important part of international capital transactions.

To recapitulate: Friedman assumes that capital movements, other than those accommodating the current account, have no permanent effect on the exchange rate and that the current account itself does not depend on asset pricing considerations. His 'fundamental' value of the exchange rate is due to commodity flow considerations only. We might call that the long-run neutrality-of-asset-pricing assumption.

Given this – completely implicit, and therefore unargued – assumption, Friedman then suggests as his perhaps most enticing, but after the introduction of flexible exchange rates evidently empirically disproved, suggestion that flexible exchange rates would also tend to stay close to their 'fundamentals'. Flexible exchange rates would very likely prove to be 'stable' exchange rates. Or, in his own words: 'Advocacy of flexible exchange rates is *not* equivalent to advocacy of unstable exchange rates. The ultimate objective is a world in which exchange rates, while *free* to vary, are in fact highly stable.'[9] This statement is part of what one could call Friedman's basic paradigm, tirelessly reiterated by him, that the politically undisturbed private enterprise system is inherently stable. In 'proving' this point in *The Case for Flexible Exchange Rates*, Friedman makes a shocking mistake in modelling, a mistake which shows that without an explicit mathematical model, at least at the back of his or her mind, the economic theoretician is liable to the most serious mistakes – a mistake astonishing in one who, as Milton Friedman, is a theoretical statistician in his own right and may be taken to be familiar with probability theory.

(At this point I should emphasize perhaps that I do not at all attack Milton Friedman on *ideological* grounds, but merely for his faulty theoretical argument. I am just as much of a classical liberal as he is; but I would never base a defence of the free enterprise system on its stability properties and not even on efficiency grounds in any abstract and *absolute* sense. I would much rather base its defence on the faults of any conceivable alternatives, and, in particular, the informational inefficiency of government. Thus I would always use a comparative argument of the type suggested by Winston Churchill, who thought democracy palpably bad but had never found a better system. Or, perhaps preferably, on the grounds of Adam Smith who made the memorable judgement: 'The statesman, who should attempt to direct private people in what manner they ought to employ their capitals' would attempt a task 'which would nowhere be so dangerous as in the hands of a man who had *folly and presumption* enough to fancy himself fit to exercise it'.[10])

Friedman's argument runs as follows:

> In general speculation is stabilizing rather than the reverse ... People who argue that speculation is generally destabilizing seldom realize that this is largely equivalent to saying that speculators lose money, *since speculation can be destabilizing in general only if speculators on the average sell when the currency is low in price and buy when it is high.*[11]

This is an in-group argument of Friedman's within the class of speculators only. If we have different groups of exchange dealers, speculators on the one hand and import and export merchants on the other, Friedman concedes that his argument no longer strictly holds:[12] 'It does not, of course, follow that speculation is not destabilizing; professional speculators might on the average make money while a changing body of amateurs regularly lost larger sums. But, while this may happen, it is hard to see why there is any presumption that it will; the presumption is rather the opposite.'[13] I, too, think this possibility irrelevant for the present, but for another reason: if 98 per cent or more of transactions in the foreign exchange markets are on capital account, the volume of transactions on current account is much too small to be successfully exploited by the group of speculators. So we have to criticize Friedman's basic point.

Let us spell it out in more detail. The alleged theorem says that *profitable speculation is price stabilizing*. For, in order to make a profit the speculator must buy, when the price is low. By buying when the price is low he tends, however, to push up the price towards its mean value, thus reducing price fluctuations and contributing to price stabilization. If he wants to make a profit he has to sell, on the other hand, when the price is high. But by selling when the price is high, he pushes the price down towards its mean, once more contributing to a reduction in price fluctuations. Profitability of speculation thus necessarily requires that the average speculator should buy when the price is low and sell when it is high; that would have the necessary consequence of price stabilization according to the rules of demand and supply theory. This – once more Marshallian – representative agent model is reinforced by the usual argument of the elimination of the unfit: speculators who act otherwise make losses and therefore will eventually have to leave the market. Thus, profitable speculation which stabilizes price fluctuations is left. A fully convincing argument and very easy to grasp, is it not?

Actually, dozens of authors since the late 1950s have tried their hand at proving it rigorously. Note that Friedman first of all implicitly assumes once again that speculation, which we might call a transaction on capital account, does not *change* the 'fundamentally' determined price in the long run. In fact, particular shapes of demand functions have to be assumed in order that the argument should fully go through. Orosel has shown that demand functions must be assumed to be *linear*.[14] But to my mind that still is not the greatest difficulty of the argument. The greatest difficulty is the information assumption behind the highly plausible sequence in the syllogism: in order to buy with a profit one has to know that the price is low; and in order to sell with a profit one has to know that the price is high. Speculators have to know the 'fundamental' average price, the 'natural' price around which the market price merely fluctuates. In his attempt to prove the existence of a 'fundamental' price for exchange rates, Friedman assumes that it exists and is known to exist, the worst kind of circular argument possible. His notion is just that of the Emperor Diocletian who was sure that a 'true' price exists and that it is a 'just' one, to boot.

There is an important theoretical model of temporal price change which is not only supported by a large body of analytical thought but also by persistent empirical evidence, which shows that the opposite is true: if prices follow what is commonly called a random walk without drift, more precisely a martingale model, then the best forecast of the future price is always the present price. In this case we can never say that a price is either high or low: it is always what it is and most likely will be in the future. And if price behaviour is a simple random walk without drift we can even prove that stock holding speculation which intends to hold stock until a given price is achieved and which has to cope with a positive marginal per period cost of a unit of stock can never be profitable: for, in this case, it is true that any other price within the admissible domain will eventually be reached with certainty; but on average it will take infinitely long until it is reached.[15] As waiting until a price is reached would thus entail infinite stock holding costs, any finite price gain whatsoever at the time of sale could, on average, never compensate for this infinite cost of waiting.

Thus, with a martingale model of price behaviour over time we cannot use Friedman's argument of price stabilizing speculation to establish the existence of a 'fundamental' price which, in this case, does not exist apart from the present price ('the market price'). On the other hand, with a 'fundamental' price Friedman's argument goes through, of course, at least under the frequently not implausible assumption of near-linear demand functions and the independence of speculative gains from interest rate changes.[16] In this case, however, it is much older than Friedman. In fact, it was treated very extensively by John Stuart Mill 102 years before Friedman.[17] Mill explains it for the case of the wheat market and the beneficial effects of corn merchants in it. Now wheat is the typical example of a fully reproducible commodity for the nineteenth century – and with respect to that I would be the last person to deny the existence of a 'fundamentally' determined price in standard textbook terms: we can assume the demand function for such a staple food to be nearly constant over time – or, at worst, only slowly changing over time, above all with changing population. We can assume that supply variations of wheat were mainly determined by the weather and, perhaps, accidentally by wars and breakdowns of transport. The existence of a 'natural' price in the sense of Smith was very close to reality. Above all, such an average wheat price was well known to a numerous class of professional grain merchants and thus informationally efficient. There, price stabilizing behaviour was therefore highly plausible. But the exchange rate is most emphatically not the wheat price. It is buffeted by much more than the easily ascertainable weather.

As for the introduction of flexible exchange rates it is now common knowledge that, contrary to the expectations of many economists, conditioned in particular by Friedman's thinking, real exchange rate volatility jumped by an order of magnitude.[18] Even more generally, Nelson Mark has recently shown in a one-and-a-quarter century study of the pound–dollar rate: 'The pattern of volatility observed across the subsamples suggests that the dynamics of the real exchange rate and associated fundamental variables may depend on the particular nominal exchange rate regime in effect.'[19]

Martingales and random walks

It is necessary to give a brief review of the basic probabilistic model behind financial markets: the martingale model and, what is frequently confounded with it in the literature, the random walk.[20]

If X is a stochastic variable whose realization at time point t has value x_t and if Δx_t is the absolute difference $x_t - x_{t-1}$, then X is said to show martingale behaviour if

$$E(x_t) = x_{t-1} \tag{2.1a}$$

$$E(\Delta x_t) = 0 \tag{2.1b}$$

In words: the expected value of x_t is just the previously achieved value x_{t-1} and its expected change is zero.

This will obviously be the case if X changes from period to period only by a random variable u_t, with mean zero and the property that u_t is independently distributed with respect to the previous realization x_{t-1}. For in this case we have:

$$x_t = 1 \cdot x_{t-1} + u_t \quad E(u_t) = 0 \tag{2.2}$$

Note that x_{t-1} in equation (2.2) has a coefficient of unity; this is therefore called the unit root case.

The variable, which is commonly examined in financial markets, is the asset price. Let us call it S. Actually, for good empirical as well as theoretical reasons, what is studied is usually the (natural) logarithm of this price, call it s_t, once more at a point in time t. Let us assume that s_t, or a transform of it, s'_t, shows martingale behaviour.

In one of his most important papers, Paul Samuelson[21] argued that in an *efficient* financial market, i.e. a market in which the price at any moment of time already fully reflects all available information up to that moment of time, the price of an asset, or rather a transformation of the price (to be explained shortly), would show martingale behaviour. Let us call ϕ_{t-1} the information set at time $t-1$. The efficient market martingale of the logarithm of the price transform, to be called s', would then be:

$$E(s'_t/\phi_{t-1}) = s'_{t-1} \tag{2.3a}$$

$$E(\Delta s'_t/\phi_{t-1}) = 0 \tag{2.3b}$$

It is important to realize that an asset price (or its logarithmic price transform) could show martingale behaviour regardless of whether the market is efficient or not. If it is not efficient we would simply have stated either an empirically correct model only or one resting on some other theoretical foundation. Thus, there is no necessary one-to-one relationship between asset price martingales and efficient markets. In other words, market efficiency is a sufficient, but not a necessary, condition for martingale behaviour.

The appropriate transformation in question is that martingale behaviour is commonly argued for the *discounted* price (though not necessarily only for the transformation, if s is the exchange rate). In an efficient market there can be full information about an expected price change as long as it cannot be used profitably in the market by any individual. Call the interest rate at time $t-1$, which is the common one-period rate of discount for all individuals, r_{t-1}. Then we have:

$$\begin{aligned} s'_t &= s_{t-1} + u_t - \ln(1 + r_{t-1}) \\ &\sim s_{t-1} + u_t - r_{t-1} \qquad \text{(for } r_{t-1} \text{ small)} \end{aligned} \tag{2.4}$$

Note that the martingale model makes a statement about the first moment of a distribution only; or, in other words, about its expected value and thus about the mean of its change. Higher moments, on the other hand, are left unspecified. The (simple) random walk differs from a martingale in two respects. First, it assumes a distribution function and therefore defines all moments, and not only the first moment. In particular it defines a specific variance of the process. In this sense it is a particular subcase of possible martingales: the class of all martingales is wider. On the other hand, a simple random walk with drift is not a martingale. So the class of all simple random walks is also wider than the class of martingales.

The simple random walk is one with discrete states (a discrete state space) in only one dimension at discrete time points and with a particular distribution function.[22] Let the logarithm of the discounted value of an asset price s'_t follow a random process over time, which describes a movement on the x-axis, and be called $X_t \equiv s'_t$. Let us, without loss of generality, assume that initially (at time point 0) the logarithm of the discounted asset price is at point zero, i.e. $s'_0 \equiv X_0 = 0$. At time $t=1$ this representation of the asset price undergoes a step or jump Z_1. (In a slightly more general case than the simple random walk, Z_1 would be a random variable having any given distribution.) At time $t=2$ the asset price representation undergoes a further jump Z_2, where Z_2 is independent of Z_1 and with the same distribution, and so on. Thus we have:

$$X_t = Z_1 + Z_2 + Z_3 + \ldots + Z_t \tag{2.5}$$

In the simple random walk we assume the following distribution function for Z_i:

$$\text{prob}(Z_i = 1 \cdot \epsilon) = p \tag{2.6a}$$

$$\text{prob}(Z_i = -1 \cdot \epsilon) = q \tag{2.6b}$$

$$\text{prob}(Z_i = 0) = 1 - p - q \qquad \epsilon > 0 \tag{2.6c}$$

Thus, during any small time interval, more exactly at the next discrete time point, the logarithm of the discounted asset price value, s'_t, can only move one unit step of length ϵ upwards or one unit step of length ϵ downwards or can stay where it is. It can *never* move by more than one unit step per period. The probability distribution generated is a multinomial probability distribution.

Each single step or jump has mean μ and variance σ^2 as follows:

$$\mu = (p - q)\epsilon \tag{2.7a}$$

$$\sigma^2 = [p + q - (p - q)^2]\epsilon^2 \tag{2.7b}$$

If our asset price movement shows an unrestricted simple random walk, the mean of s'_T, that is to say after T periods when having started at $s'_0 = 0$, is just the sum of the T means for a single step or jump, and, as the steps or jumps are independently and identically distributed, the variance is the sum over the T variances. Thus:

$$E(s'_T) = T\mu = T(p - q) \cdot \epsilon \tag{2.8a}$$

$$\text{Var}(s'_T) = T\sigma^2 = T[p + q - (p - q)^2]\,\epsilon^2 \tag{2.8b}$$

Note that for the unrestricted simple random walk the variance of the transformed asset price goes to infinity with $T \to \infty$ and increases proportionately with time. Note, furthermore, that the mean change per unit of time, μ, is the drift of the simple random walk. In the case of a martingale, the random walk has to be driftless, i.e. $p = q$. In this case the mean jump is, of course, $\mu = 0$ and the variance $\sigma^2 = 2p \cdot \epsilon^2$. The variance of the transformed asset price once more goes towards infinity with time. Let us quote the textbook of Cox and Miller on the particularly interesting latter case (note that they call our variable a ‘particle’):[23]

> When $p = q$ the behaviour of the particle is somewhat singular. It follows from our results that starting from state 0, the particle reaches any other given state with probability one, but that the mean time to achieve this passage is infinite. Having reached the given state it will return to state 0 with probability one, again with infinite mean passage time. Thus an unrestricted particle, if allowed sufficient time, is certain to make indefinitely large excursions from its starting point and is also certain to return to its starting point.

We shall need this fact later on when discussing exchange rate movements. And we have used it already: in this 'standard' case, stock holding speculation with stock held costing anything but zero per period can never be profitable because, in order to wait for any given price, stock will have to be held on average for an infinitely long period.

The stochastic process with a continuous state space, which 'corresponds' to the simple random walk without drift, more precisely the limiting process when letting step-length go to zero, is called Brownian motion.

What is the probability for a variable following a random walk and starting at state a ever to become zero? If p either equals q or is smaller than q, the probability is one (as stated above). Only if p, the probability to move away from zero, is larger than q, the probability ever to reach 0 is smaller than one. In this case the probability never to reach 0 when starting out at state a and a step length of ϵ, let us call it N, is given as follows:

$$N = 1 - \left(\frac{q}{p}\right)^{\frac{a}{\epsilon}} \tag{2.9}$$

This important formula has many financial market implications. Let us briefly discuss three.

First, if the rate of interest R to be paid per period on the capital of a firm is given by $q \cdot \epsilon$ (a fixed percentage of initial capital each period), while the rate of profit varies stochastically and is on average $p \cdot \epsilon$, once more a given percentage of initial capital per period, then any firm with a finite wholly borrowed initial capital with logarithm a/ϵ will certainly go broke, that is reach the state of the logarithm of capital zero (at which we assume it has to be wound up), unless $p > q$. Firms thus have to earn higher rates of profit than the interest they pay on their capital in order to survive.

Second, assume that the real rate of profit in enterprises, let us once more make it out to be $p \cdot \epsilon$, is determined solely by the obvious 'fundamentals', the stochastic flow of profits from innovation and the risk preferences of entrepreneurs. Let us then deduce the real rate of interest in the economy derived from the interest which innovating entrepreneurs can pay their banks on their borrowed capital. Then we can make a doubly Schumpeterian point. *One*: without innovation there would be a zero real rate of interest (of course, we have then endorsed the problematic notion of Schumpeter that there is no other source of interest). But much more important is *two*: the real rate of interest is not only determined 'fundamentally'. The expected real rate of interest in the economy, or the return the banks actually achieve on average, to be called R, is the following (assuming the banks lend the firms all their capital, which is always of size $a \cdot \epsilon$, assuming furthermore that they get nothing when the firm goes broke, and assuming finally that they charge a bank rate of interest $B = q \cdot \epsilon$ while the stochastic real rate of profit is $p \cdot \epsilon$):

$$R = B \cdot \left[1 - \left(\frac{q}{p} \right)^{\frac{a}{\epsilon}} \right] \tag{2.10}$$

That is to say the actually realized real rate of interest depends, besides technical and preference variables, negatively on the stochastic variability of the returns on innovation and also negatively on the amount of capital which banks allow innovating firms, in other words: on the amount of credit rationing. Thus, real interest will normally fall quite a bit short of what is technically possible and what the risk preference of entrepreneurs would allow. Even the real rate of interest depends upon financial market conditions! It will be relatively the lower, the greater credit rationing is and the more variable over time the returns from given innovations are. Not only are classical economic models long-run and ignore the large class of services where supply arises at demand without any additional inputs, they are also limiting cases of infinite finance or liquidity.

Third, we can draw a very interesting conclusion about the necessary reserves a central bank with a fixed exchange rate has to hold, if it has determined some optimum probability of never running out of reserves and wishes to keep this probability constant during the growth of world trade.[24]

Of course, it cannot have any other than a probability of one of losing all its reserves unless its rate of inflow of reserves p is larger than its rate of outflow q.

If the probability of an inflow of reserves to the bank is p and the probability of an outflow is q, $p > q$, while the amount of each inflow is (in logarithms) always exactly ϵ, a growth of the inflow and outflow stream has, surprisingly in the face of the well-known treatment of monetary flows in quantity theory, two completely different effects depending on whether only the number of transactions per unit of time changes or whether only the average size of each transaction changes. More frequent inflows as well as outflows do not change the necessary reserves at all! That is to say, if the rate of inflows per period changes from p to $\lambda \cdot p$ and the rate of outflows also changes from q to $\lambda \cdot q$, $\lambda > 0$, the probability of losing all reserves, $(1 - (q/p)^{a/\epsilon})$, given a and ϵ, does not change at all. Thus, the required reserves relative to a proportionate change of both q and p are zero. If, on the other hand the average size or volume of each outflow or inflow transaction changes proportionately from ϵ to $\lambda \cdot \epsilon$, $\lambda > 0$, then reserves, too, have to change proportionately by that factor λ, from a to λa, in order to keep the probability of losing all reserves constant. The elasticity of required reserves relative to a change in the volume of each transaction then is unity, which is the elasticity which the quantity equation of money makes us think is always necessary in case of financial reserves. A change in the average number of transactions thus works on desired reserves completely differently from their change in size. In the case of the desired exchange reserves during growth of world trade, this is likely to mean that real increases in exports and imports over time, which are above all increases in the number of transactions, increase our reserve requirements very little. Inflation, on the other hand, is likely to entail a proportionate increase in desired nominal reserves because it makes the nominal payment for unchanged real export and import items proportionately larger, as a first approximation. Thus, real growth works quite differently from nominal growth, an aspect once more clouded when we look at the quantity equation of money. The same is also likely to be true for capital transactions, with which we are mainly concerned here: they are likely to be large transactions and, on average, they tend to become ever larger during growth of world trade. Therefore they make a proportionate increase of reserves desirable.

These are only a few examples of the important conclusions to be drawn when explicitly modelling financial transactions as stochastic processes and the wealth of insights to be gained already from the simple random walk. We had better get accustomed to thinking in their terms.

Some exchange rate empirics

But do martingales, and in particular simple random walks, have anything to do with the actual empirics of the cosmos of the exchange rate? The simple answer is: yes, very much so indeed.[25]

In a seminal article from 1983, Meese and Rogoff[26] have shown that the exchange rates of the great world currencies cannot be distinguished for shorter time horizons from what they called a random walk.

To put it more precisely, they showed that very many types of then current exchange rate models – in fact, with hardly any exaggeration we might say 'all' models – showed no better forecasting behaviour than a 'no change forecast', in spite of the fact that they might explain exchange rates quite well within sample; and they showed this for time horizons of one month, six months and twelve months. Actually, what they thus tested was deviation from a martingale, as higher moments of forecasts were not examined. Their finding has become 'orthodox' wisdom[27] and by some is still thought not to have been disproved so far, though many have tried: 'beating a random walk' has become something of a parlour game among exchange rate econometricians. It is true that in a well-known article, Nelson Mark[28] has claimed to have found a type of model superior to the 'random walk without drift' (i.e. more correctly, the martingale). But his model is dubious, in the first place, as it rests on unsound econometric foundations.[29] And second it encompasses one quarter of a year, four quarters, eight quarters and sixteen quarters, thus extending in the latter two instances (as its title intimates) beyond the period examined by Meese and Rogoff. It is commonly agreed among applied exchange rate theorists that for periods *longer* than one year there *is* some hope of finding rather

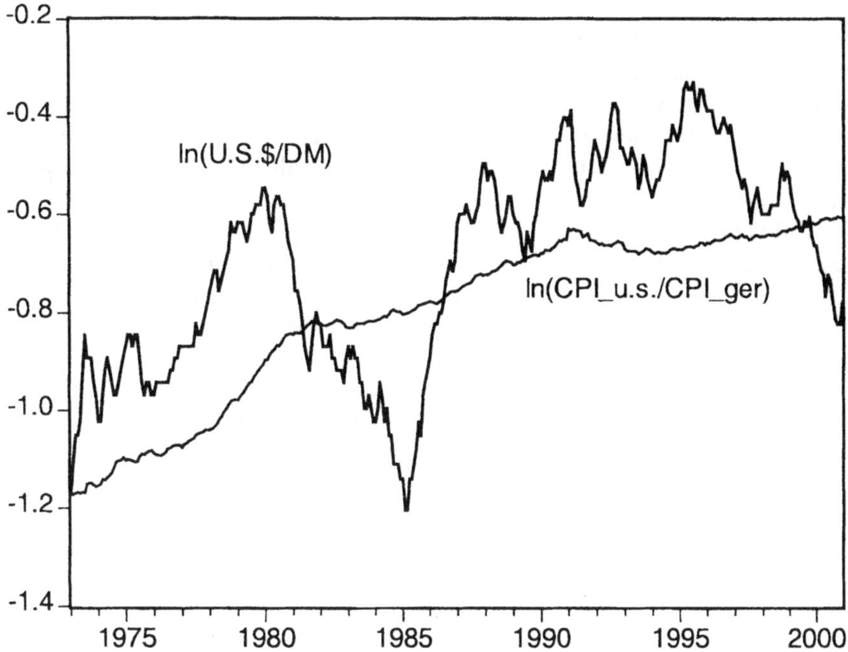

Figure 2.1 US dollars in terms of Deutsche Marks.

Is there a mean reverting tendency of the dollar or was there just a regime shift at the end of the 1990s? At least the US-dollar remained undervalued relative to its purchasing power parity for a decade or so.

weak, but not completely useless, explanatory exchange rate equations. And this appears to be the consensus of exchange rate practitioners as well, who nowadays tend to have substantial training in theoretical economics: up to an horizon of one year they tend to use mechanical ('chartist') forecasting techniques while for periods longer than one year they tend to turn to models called 'fundamental'.

Recently, there is very promising work by Ronald MacDonald[30] at the IMF, with numerous collaborators, especially at the IMF. His models are nonlinear in logarithms in the sense of being error correction models. All models so far considered in theory as being 'fundamental' (of which more later), are, however, linear in logarithms. In this sense MacDonald-type models are 'unorthodox', or, perhaps better, innovative. Even considering his models, we can therefore say that, up to one year, exchange rates behave in a way that is statistically indistinguishable from a martingale, taking linear fundamental models as a measuring rod. Thus, they have a very strong short-run stochastic component, which might partially wash out in the longer run.

It has to be admitted though that, in recent years, the predictability of exchange rates seems to improve somewhat. The MacDonald–Marsh model (which seems to be by far the best available) exhibited improved performance during the 1990s.[31] And, in one Master's thesis after another, my students in Vienna seem to be routinely able to 'beat a random walk' for the post-1987 period and the main developed countries' exchange rates with numerous variants of the basic MacDonald–Taylor model experimented with.[32]

Looking at higher moments than the first, it is actually well known that exchange rates do not exhibit random walk behaviour. There is agreement that over long horizons the variance of real exchange rates does not increase linearily over time. Furthermore, random walks would show not only independently distributed, but also identically distributed 'steps' or 'jumps'. It is well known that all prices of financial assets 'go through protracted quiet periods and equally protracted turbulent periods';[33] in other words, that they have periods of low variance and periods of high variance, which contradicts the random walk assumption of identically distributed 'error' terms. We can model these changing variances either by assuming that the stochastic term has normal distribution around a trend which at times jumps according to a Poisson distribution;[34] or by a Markov-switching process from a state with low variance to one with high.[35] The practical problem is that it is very difficult to forecast these changes in variances. It has been suggested that they might occur when changes in governments are reasonably to be expected.[36] This may be true. But there are many other possibilities of a major shift in previous market conditions to which participants have first to get accustomed. More or less in desperation, a recent study concluded: 'Macroeconomics is an inessential piece of the exchange rate volatility puzzle.'[37]

Over longer periods it is difficult to find consistent autocorrelation patterns of relative exchange rate changes; and, indeed, if they were to exist, exchange rates would then deviate consistently from the martingale. For if the coefficient of autocorrelation is ρ and the (logarithm of the) variable in question is x, first order autocorrelation would be defined by (equation 2.11a) and the change of x, as (equation 2.11b) shows, would differ from zero:

$$x_t = \rho x_{t-1} + \epsilon_t,\ E(\epsilon_t) = 0,\ i.i.d., \tag{2.11a}$$

$$E(\Delta x_t) = -(1-\rho)x_{t-1} \neq 0 \tag{2.11b}$$

However, there seem to be subperiods (years) when a given exchange rate either goes up or goes down comparatively consistently, which would imply positive autocorrelation. Furthermore, changes of exchange rates deemed 'excessive' by the market are frequently reversed, which would imply negative autocorrelation. Technical buying and selling rules can try to exploit subperiods, when this occurs.[38]

There is an important study by MacDonald and Marsh[39] which found by direct questioning that exchange rate dealers use quite different forecasting models and, even more surprisingly, that some are 'better' than others in the sense that they make persistent gains. Very revealingly, these successful traders are successful, however, usually only in one single exchange rate. This contradicts efficiency of the market from a microeconomic point of view. Furthermore, certain exchange rates, even of the large international currencies, show persistent trends. By itself, this would not yet contradict the martingale model: in an efficient market, only the suitably discounted log of the exchange rate would have to show martingale behaviour. However, the trends tend to differ substantially from the suitable discount factors. This would contradict efficiency, but could easily be explained by a lack of risk neutrality of the 'average' market participant, as, in fact, we shall argue. However, the relevant risk aversion measure is usually both large, and also frequently shows substantial variability not easily to be explained. The data therefore suggest that foreign exchange markets are not efficient, but show short to medium-run behaviour indistinguishable from a martingale, nevertheless.

Monetarists would consider purchasing power parity (PPP) the 'fundamental' for exchange rates; and, indeed, this was the 'fundamental' assumed by Milton Friedman in 1950.[40] PPP argues that, by goods market arbitrage, exchange rates should adjust in such a way as to make the same quantity of any tradeable service or commodity equally costly in money terms. For very long sample periods, adjustment of exchange rates to PPP has been shown to work, but only extremely slowly: 'half-lives' of deviations from PPP generally work out at some three to four years. Half-lives are, however, quite undemanding measures of conformity to the 'fundamental' theory; if we take the normal statistical measure of significance, a 95 per cent adjustment to the PPP value, then this would imply an adjustment period of some fifteen to twenty years, on some calculations even more.[41] This is what has been memorably termed the 'purchasing power parity puzzle',[42] (PPPP or 'four-P' for short). Even worse, no study has yet been able to prove at all a tendency towards PPP for the large financial currencies of countries with little inflation after 1973, when flexible exchange rates were introduced.[43] Or should we rather say for the period of re-introduction of convertibility on capital account and the concomitant international capital mobility? For inflating currencies, a tendency towards PPP can be shown, but only when currencies are sufficiently far away from it.

Thus there is very weak empirical evidence for what some still consider the most 'fundamental' exchange rate explanation. There is none whatsoever for the second 'fundamental' explanation, the asset market equilibrium of uncovered interest parity, if linear equations are used. Interest rates usually just do not show up in log-linear equations, or do so with the wrong sign.[44] It will be one of our main points, however, that this is only to be expected theoretically and is just due to faulty modelling.

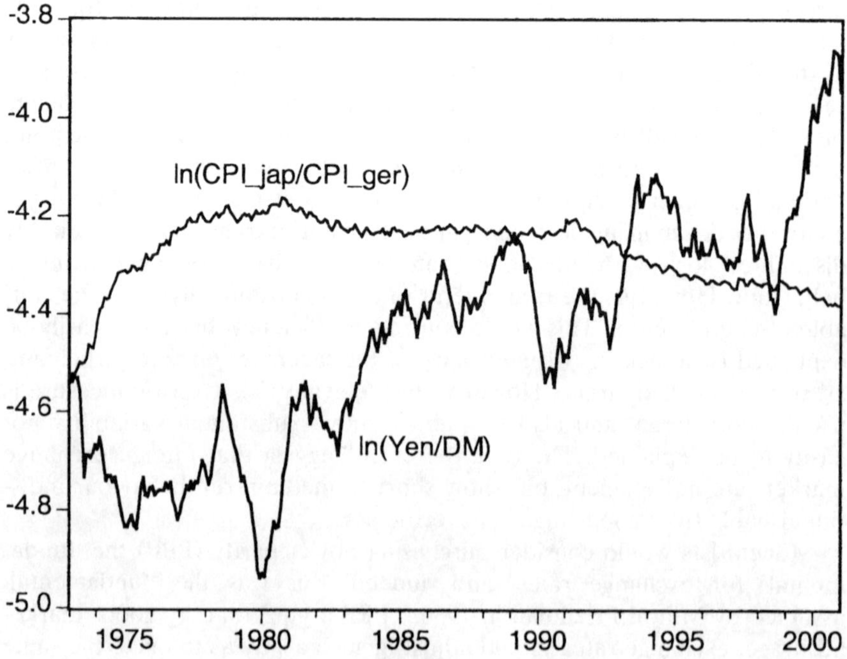

Figure 2.2 Yens in terms of Deutsche Marks.

The yen seems to have been overvalued relative to its purchasing power parity for long periods. The exchange rate develops quite differently to the purchasing power parity.

Another well-established empirical fact is that real exchange rates and nominal exchange rates do not differ substantially and tend to have the same variance. This once more runs counter to common theory.

Disquieting for advocates of flexible exchange rates is the fact that exchange rate variance is regime-specific and that, as has been pointed out already,[45] both nominal and real exchange rates showed higher variability post-Bretton Woods (post 1973) than before. The introduction of flexible exchange rates, contrary to M. Friedman's argument, proved to increase exchange rate variability by an order of magnitude, if not by even more.

Finally, it can be shown that in many countries exchange rate movements cause changes particularly in the long-run real interest rates.[46] The dollar–Deutsche Mark exchange rate, for example, has caused (in a statistical sense, i.e. 'Granger-caused') variations in the real long-run German interest rate. It is very important to keep this in mind. It does not exactly contradict the theory as such, but, as to the direction of causation, it decidedly runs counter to the usual interpretation of uncovered interest parity.

There are many more empirical exchange rate puzzles, some of which will be taken up in the remaining lectures. For now, suffice it to say that, with exchange rates, the data are so wide of the mark from the usual theoretical predictions that they justify a radical re-examination of exchange rate theory.

Notes

1 Milton Friedman, 'The Case for Flexible Exchange Rates' (originally 1950), in: M. Friedman, *Essays in Positive Economics*, Chicago 1953, pp. 157–203, here p. 157f.
2 Eugen Ritter Boehm von Bawerk, 'Unsere passive Handelsbilanz', in: F.X. Weiss (ed.), *Gesammelte Schriften von Eugen von Böhm-Bawerk*, Vienna–Leipzig 1924, pp. 499–515.
3 Implied rather than explicitly stated in Robert E. Mundell, *International Economics*, New York–London 1968, ch. 18 (and originally in his 1963 article in the *Canadian Journal of Economics*).
4 Rita Landauer, *Kausalitätsanalyse zwischen kurzfristigen Zinssätzen und Wechselkursen (DM zu Yen, US-$ und Pfund Sterling)*, Master's thesis, University of Vienna, 1998. Ronald MacDonald, 'Exchange Rate Behaviour: Are Fundamentals Important?', *Economic Journal*, 109 (1999a), 673–91, thinks that even inflation rates are affected (p. 684): 'Disequilibrium in either the yen–dollar or mark–dollar markets not only affects "own" inflation and interest rates but also the inflation rate and interest rates in the other system.'
5 For the case of the Bundesbank see Richard Clarida and Mark Gertler, 'How the Bundesbank Conducts Monetary Policy', in: Christina D. and David H. Romer, *Reducing Inflation – Motivation and Strategy*, Chicago–London 1997, ch. 10, pp. 363–412, esp. pp. 382, 387f., 390.
6 James E. Meade, *The Balance of Payments* (*The Theory of Economic Policy*, vol. one), London etc. 1954, p. 11f.
7 Friedman (1953), op. cit., p. 183.
8 If p is the price and q the quantity, and t is time, any value $p \cdot q$ changes in relative terms over time as follows:

$$\frac{d(p \cdot q)}{dt} \cdot \frac{1}{pq} = \frac{\frac{dp}{dt} \cdot q}{pq} + \frac{\frac{dq}{dt} \cdot p}{pq} = \frac{dp}{dt} \cdot \frac{1}{p} + \frac{dq}{dt} \cdot \frac{1}{q}$$

9 Friedman (1953), op. cit., p. 158.
10 Smith *WN* (1776), IV.ii.10.
11 Friedman (1953), op. cit., p. 175; my emphasis added.
12 See also William J. Baumol, 'Speculation, Profitability, and Stability', *Review of Economics and Statistics*, 39 (1957), 263–71.
13 Friedman (1953), op. cit., p. 175.
14 Gerhard O. Orosel, 'Profitable Speculation and Price Stability', *Jahrbücher für Nationalökonomie und Statistik*, 199 (1984), 485–501.
15 See Lecture IV, p. 78f.
16 For a new version of the influence of speculation which, though assuming a 'fundamental' value of the exchange, derives different results from Friedman see: John A. Carlson and C.L. Osler, 'Rational Speculators and Exchange Rate Volatility', *European Economic Review*, 44 (2000), 231–53.
17 John Stuart Mill, *Principles of Political Economy with Some of their Applications*

to Social Philosophy, London 1848, Book IV, ch. 11, §§4 and 5 (vol. II, pp. 254–61 of the original edition).

18 A study by Mussa is generally credited with having at long last conclusively demonstrated this fact: Michael Mussa, 'Nominal Exchange Rate Regimes and the Behavior of Real Exchange Rates: Evidence and Implications', *Carnegie–Rochester Conference Series on Public Policy*, 25 (Autumn 1986), pp. 117–213. Mussa found a variance of the change of the logarithm of the real exchange rate 'generally eight to eighty times greater in 1973–83 than ... in 1957–70' (p. 149).

19 Nelson C. Mark, 'Fundamentals of the Real Dollar–Pound Rate: 1871–1994', in: R. MacDonald and J.L. Stein (eds), *Equilibrium Exchange Rates*, Boston etc. 1999, pp. 191–208, here p. 197.

20 In my exposition I follow at first largely Stephen F. LeRoy, 'Efficient Capital Markets and Martingales', *Journal of Economic Literature*, 27 (Dec. 1989), 1583–621.

21 Paul A. Samuelson, 'Proof That Properly Anticipated Prices Fluctuate Randomly', *Industrial Management*, 6 (1965), 41–9.

22 For the exposition of the random walk I follow D.R. Cox and H.D. Miller, *The Theory of Stochastic Processes*, London 1965.

23 Ibid. p. 38f.

24 What follows is a brief sketch of some of the main points I made in Erich Streissler, 'A Stochastic Model of International Reserve Requirements During Growth of World Trade', *Zeitschrift für Nationalökonomie*, 29 (1969), 347–70, the second part of my Inaugural Lecture in Vienna.

25 For recent surveys of exchange rate empirics see especially Kenneth A. Froot and Kenneth Rogoff, 'Perspectives on PPP and Long-Run Real Exchange Rates' and Jeffrey A. Frankel and Andrew K. Rose, 'Empirical Research on Nominal Exchange Rates', both in: S.M. Grossman and K. Rogoff (eds), *Handbook of International Economics*, vol. III, Amsterdam etc. 1995, ch. 32, pp. 1647–88, and ch. 33, pp. 1689–729. Furthermore Ronald MacDonald, 'What Do We Really Know About Real Exchange Rates?', in: R. MacDonald and J.M. Stein (eds), *Equilibrium Exchange Rates*, Boston etc. 1999, pp. 19–65.

26 Richard A. Meese and Kenneth Rogoff, 'Empirical Exchange Rate Models of the Seventies – Do They Fit Out of Sample?', *Journal of International Economics*, 14 (1983), 3–24.

27 About the same time Mussa (1986), op. cit., also concludes: 'Nominal exchange rates or their logarithms are well-described as following random walks' (p. 199).

28 Nelson C. Mark, 'Exchange Rates and Fundamentals: Evidence on Long-Horizon Predictability', *American Economic Review*, 85 (1995), 201–18.

29 In estimating the 'fundamentals-determined' value of the nominal exchange rate, Mark restricts the coefficients of the home and foreign log money variables to 1 and –1 respectively. This misspecifies the model econometrically, introducing spurious regression. Simon Quijano, *Can Movements in Emerging Market Currencies be Explained Using Fundamentals-Based Exchange Rate Models?* Doctoral Dissertation, University of Vienna 2000, has re-estimated the Mark model for Thailand in Appendix I and shows that the model can apparently forecast better and better the longer the time horizon (just as in the original article by Mark), but that its Durbin–Watson Ratio also falls monotonically towards zero!

30 Ronald MacDonald and Mark P. Taylor, 'The Monetary Model of the Exchange Rate: Long Run Relationships, Short Run Dynamics and How to Beat a Random Walk', *Journal of International Money and Finance*, 13 (1994),

276–90; Ronald MacDonald, 'Exchange Rate Behaviour: Are Fundamentals Important?', *Economic Journal*, 109 (1999a), 660–72.

31 See Ronald MacDonald and Ian Marsh, *Exchange Rate Modelling*, Boston etc. 1999.

32 MacDonald (1999a), op. cit. attributes that mainly to a change in econometric techniques. He says (p. 682) the finding of Meese and Rogoff 'is no longer valid in the light of new econometric methods for addressing issues of simultaneity and dynamic interactions'. I think the undoubted difference is rather due to changes in reaction patterns with the ever mounting importance of international capital movements.

33 LeRoy (1989), op. cit., p. 1590.

34 Clifford A. Ball and Antonio Roma, 'A Jump Diffusion Model for the European Monetary System', *Journal of International Money and Finance*, 12 (1993), 475–92; similarly Horst Kräger and Peter Kugler, 'Non-linearities in Foreign Exchange Markets: a Different Perspective', *Journal of International Money and Finance*, 12 (1993), 195–208.

35 John R. Freeman, Jude C. Hays and Helmut Stix, 'Democracy and Markets: The Case of Exchange Rates', *Working Paper* 39, Oesterreichische Nationalbank, Vienna 1999.

36 Ibid.

37 Robert P. Flood and Andrew K. Rose, 'Understanding Exchange Rate Volatility Without the Contrivance of Macroeconomics', *Economic Journal*, 109 (1999), 660–72, here p. 662 (in italics). The authors' definition of macroeconomics appears somewhat narrow to me, however.

38 Martin Buchner, *Markteffizienz und mechanische Verfahren der Spekulation am Beispiel der USD/DM und USD/JPY Wechselkurse*, Master's thesis, University of Vienna 2000, demonstrates that not only daily changes but also runs of successive days of exchange rates show leptokurtosis. Thus, unusually long runs can be utilized by chartist methods.

39 Ronald MacDonald and Ian W. Marsh, 'Currency Forecasters are Heterogeneous: Confirmation and Consequences', *Journal of International Money and Finance*, 15 (1996), 665–85.

40 See note 1.

41 Actually, 'half-lives' are not half the *time period* it takes until a given deviation is eliminated, for in the models used this time is always infinity, theoretically speaking. Half-lives are much rather the time it takes until one half of the initial deviation is estimated as being eliminated. This triviality seems to be misunderstood even by Ronald MacDonald when, after having found a half-life of four years, he repeatedly speaks of 'around eight years' as the total adjustment period (see MacDonald and Stein (1999), op. cit., pp. 28, 209). My calculation of the 95 per cent limit would make that time span out to be more than 17 years.

42 Kenneth Rogoff, 'The Purchasing Power Parity Puzzle', *Journal of Economic Literature*, 34 (1996), 647–68.

43 Frequently convergence to PPP can be shown only in case of large deviations from this norm, not for small deviations. See, e.g. MacDonald (1999b), op. cit., p. 34, who states: 'Real exchange rates behave like random walks for small deviations from PPP, but are strongly mean reverting for large (positive or negative) deviations.' With the present, very low inflation rates in all the major most developed countries, the consequent minute inflation differences seem to drop out of the picture altogether, as far as understanding exchange rate changes is concerned, e.g. Anish Gupta, *How to Beat the Random Walk – The German Mark and the Italian Lira: Exchange Rate Models Revisited*, Master's thesis, University of Vienna 1999, does not find statistically significant

convergence of the real exchange rates named to PPP relative to the dollar since 1977. The real exchange rate movement cannot be distinguished from a random walk, which is surprising for the lira.

44 For recent evidence for mainly the 'wrong' interest coefficient see, e.g. Ronald MacDonald, 'What Determines Real Exchange Rates? The Long and the Short of It', in MacDonald and Stein (1999), op. cit., pp. 241–84, here pp. 271ff., and also his remark on another paper on p. 50 of that book (quoted as 1999c).

45 See notes 18 and 19.

46 See Landauer, op. cit.

Lecture III Equilibria?

Interest parity and purchasing power parity – which kind of equilibria?

Purchasing power parity

'There is no logical story explaining how the change in money will cause a shift from one equilibrium to another,' Fischer Black dared to announce.[1] He added: 'There is a real international equilibrium that is largely unaffected by price levels or monetary policy'.[2] Is that true of exchange rates as well?

Established exchange rate theory provides us with two equilibrium theories of exchange rates, totally convincing on theoretical grounds (at least at first sight), but, as was pointed out already, unfortunately just as much wide of the mark empirically.

The first equilibrium theory, time-honoured, is purchasing power parity, (PPP). The argument runs as follows: one and the same commodity has to cost exactly the same in two different markets, under the following four conditions: no transport cost, no policy barrier, no differential transaction cost, but full information. For if it were otherwise, arbitrage transactions would be profitable and through them prices would rapidly be equalized. If the two markets are in different currency areas, price equalization entails that after exchanging one currency for the other, the price still has to be the same. So if the exchange rate of the two currencies against each other is permitted to vary, that is, if we have perfectly flexible exchange rates, the exchange rates should move in such a way that the price in the two markets still becomes equal. What is true for one single homogeneous commodity should also hold for a bundle of such homogeneous commodities. The same sum of money should buy the same bundle of goods everywhere: that would be purchasing power parity. And as today we have highly integrated commodity markets within the OECD countries – with, for many goods, namely the 'tradeable goods', low transport costs, hardly any political barriers, ever better information and no discernible differences in transaction costs – the conformity to purchasing power parity should hold even for aggregate bundles of goods. It should hold even for slightly heterogeneous commodities, as long as those are close substitutes. And in our modern world it should hold ever more closely, especially as information becomes ever more perfect by means of the Internet.

If we define the exchange rate S (for 'spot rate') as the sum in the home currency needed to buy one (or more usually: one hundred) units of foreign currency, i.e. as home currency divided by foreign currency, and if the price of commodity i is P_i in 'home' in units of home currency, while it is P_i^* in 'foreign' in units of foreign currency (starred prices and quantities here and always denoting foreign prices and quantities), the equilibrium condition of purchasing power parity says ('≡' stands for a definition or identity):

$$\frac{P_i}{\text{unit home currency}} = \frac{P_i^*}{\text{unit foreign currency}} \tag{3.1a}$$

$$S \equiv \frac{\text{units home currency}}{\text{one unit foreign currency}} \tag{3.1b}$$

Taking (3.1a) and (3.1b) together, we get:

$$S = \frac{P_i}{P_i^*} \tag{3.2}$$

What holds true for any one commodity should, with given quantity weights, hold true for the average of prices, the general price level, which we call P for home and P^* for foreign. Since, by arbitrage, purchasing power parity should hold for any two commodities, as long as they are internationally tradeable, i.e. as long as, in particular, their transport costs are not too high, we can take any price level, as long as it is one in tradeables. Purchasing power parity should hold whichever price level we take. We get:

$$S = \frac{P}{P^*} \tag{3.3}$$

Four important points are worth discussing.

One: when purchasing power parity theory was more fully developed in the interwar period, Haberler (1933) rightly emphasized that by its very arbitrage logic it can only hold for tradeable commodities and services.[3] But, we have to add, even for these it will actually hold only more or less strictly: for normally there are some transport costs, even with tradeables, though these are not high enough to preclude trade if the interlocal price difference is sufficiently large. Thus we can define commodity export and import points, similar to the well-known gold export and import points. This means, however, that tradeables cannot be defined by means of technical properties alone, but are dependent on price and location. It also implies (what is true in fact, too) that purchasing power parity is much more likely to hold in continental Europe than for the USA, separated by oceans from much of the rest of the world. To take an example: hair cuts are typically quoted as an obvious example of non-tradeables; but many Austrians from Eastern Austria habitually have their hair cut in Hungary. On the other hand, the best car price within the European Union was searched for even before the introduction of the euro. Thus, not only transport costs, but also lack of information counts against PPP. In the latter example it is not the lack of locational distance, but much rather the high price relative to average budgets which is likely to make PPP work, as search costs will normally be undertaken only in the case of costly items. Search costs are similar to transport cost.

Thus, purchasing power deviations are much more likely to be corrected for large price deviations than for small price deviations and much rather for costly goods than for goods the yearly consumption of which is small relative to average budgets.

Two: after Haberler (1933) had correctly stated that the PPP-price level should refer to tradeables only, more specifically one for export and import goods only, he made the (nowadays grievous) mistake of stating that one could take the consumer price level anyhow, because the consumer price level and that for tradeables will move closely in step.[4] But that is correct only if both wages and productivities move 'in step', that is, proportionately in the same way in all sectors of the economy; and if, furthermore, prices respond to cost changes at the same rate everywhere in each economy, that is, if mark-ups stay constant in relative terms. In defence of Haberler one might remark that he may have been approximately correct for the depressed and near stationary economies around the year 1933. But his notion is certainly no longer correct today.

If wages rise to the same extent in all sectors (which has happened in a number of economies, particularly in Austria) and if productivity also increases very strongly, we would typically have the following picture: labour productivity rises less in many service sectors and also in the building trades, which typically produce non-tradeables. Non-tradeables are less exposed to competition than tradeables, just because they are non-tradeables and there are fewer substitutes available. For the first-named reason, during economic growth labour costs will rise in the non-tradeables sector as compared to tradeables; for the second reason, mark-ups are likely to increase in the non-tradeables sector, so that relative prices will rise there even more than relative labour costs. *Ceteris paribus*, all this will hold the more, the more rapidly economies grow. For with higher growth the variance of productivity growth will increase. This has to be so, as for purely technical reasons there are always some sectors where labour productivity cannot increase (musicians cannot play their pieces of music faster just because their pay rises; and hospital treatment or old age treatment requires a certain amount of care, i.e. labour input, per patient – and that may even be rising with economic growth). So, for a given higher rate of average productivity the top-ranking sectors (in terms of productivity growth) have to have an even higher growth rate of productivity growth relative to the mean. Furthermore, the higher the rate of income growth, the higher the mark-up on cost is likely to be in the many non-tradeable subsectors where demand is income-elastic, as it is typically with personal services. In other words, optimal monopolistic prices will rise as a multiple of marginal cost because price elasticity tends to decline during rapid growth in sectors with income-elastic demand. For these reasons consumer price levels, which include services, are likely to rise more than the price index of tradeables only. And they will rise most in the more rapidly growing country. Therefore, rapidly growing countries show an exchange rate, which, if consumer prices are taken, will appreciate relative to purchasing power parity, if this is measured in terms of the consumer price index. Empirically, this is likely to be the case, the discussion above stating variants of the well-known Balassa–Samuelson effect.

Three: purchasing power parities frequently tend to be calculated not bilaterally, but with respect to the trade-weighted 'effective' exchange rate with respect to all countries. This is frequently done for the dollar because, thus, the empirical fit of PPP is somewhat improved. The better fit is evidently due to the fact that the USA trade to a substantial degree with highly inflationary Latin American countries where price differences soon become so very large that some adjustment has to take place. This is a subterfuge, nevertheless: by the arbitrage argument, purchasing power parity has to hold towards each and every other currency, and, in fact, every single commodity within each currency area. According to the theory it has to hold *bilaterally* and not only on the average towards selected trading partners.

Four: purchasing power parity is an equilibrium relationship devoid of any necessary unidirectional causality. Normally, it is stated that exchange rates adjust to prices. PPP is then an exchange rate theory for flexible exchange rates or for determining the necessary changes in parities for fixed exchange rates. But, particularly in the case of credibly fixed exchange rates, it will be the prices (and wages!) that have to adjust so as to make it hold. In fact, it was the innovative policy idea in Austria from about the mid-1970s, and more closely from 1981 onwards, to use the exchange rate as an instrument to influence prices. That was the so-called 'hard currency policy' of Austria, and it was a very successful policy (of course, you need 'accommodating' trade-union behaviour). Such a policy reverses the usually assumed causality structure of PPP. But as such, it is not at all unusual historically. PPP should hold even more closely within one and the same currency, e.g. at present in the euro-area, more closely because here there are no political barriers, and informational asymmetries are smaller. And, after all, economists frequently test PPP now by extending their time series back into the classical gold standard era, which provided something close to a single currency. This is perfectly legitimate, though there should be some noticeable break in the series when switching to another currency regime as this tends to change information as well as expectations and pricing behaviour. But in these cases the direction of causality may also switch.

As even prices of the same or similar commodities (close substitutes) will deviate from each other by transport cost, absolute purchasing power parity, described in equation (3.3), is not likely to hold precisely. If export and import points for any commodity are a fixed percentage of their value, then the possible deviation of prices – or of exchange rates – from PPP should remain within a fixed percentage as well. Assume therefore that exchange rates deviate from PPP by a fixed percentage. This would lead to the notion of relative purchasing power parity: if one price level remains fixed, the percentage change of exchange rates should equal the weighted percentage change of prices. In order to linearize the equation (and in conformity with monetarist practice in linearizing the quantity equation of money), (natural) logarithms of the exchange rate are usually employed. Let us call the logarithm of the exchange rate s, i.e. $\ln S \equiv s$.

We then have (3.4) instead of (3.3) as the equation of absolute purchasing power parity:

$$s = \ln P - \ln P^* \tag{3.4}$$

Let us now take differences of these logarithms. Let us call Δ_t a *time* difference between two logarithms at different points of time and Δ_l a *locational* difference of two logarithms at the same point of time, but at different places. Time differences between logarithms are equivalent to percentage changes. (To be quite precise: this is true only for infinitesimally small changes, but it is a good approximation even for larger changes.) Let us then define p as the percentage change of the price level, i.e. $p \equiv \Delta_t \ln P$, $p^* \equiv \Delta_t \ln P^*$. Thus, p and p^* are the rates of inflation, in terms of the price levels considered. Relative purchasing power parity then says:

$$\Delta_t s = p - p^* = \Delta_l p \tag{3.5}$$

In words: the percentage change of the exchange rate is the difference between the rates of inflation, measured in terms of the relevant price levels for the two currencies, that of home and that of foreign. Note an important empirical fact: the coefficient of the inflation difference in the exchange rate change equation forecast by relative purchasing power parity is *unity*.

If we look one period ahead with rational expectations we can also say: according to relative purchasing power parity, the *expected* change in the exchange rate has to equal the expected difference in inflation rates one period ahead.

As a rise in the exchange rate is in this notation a depreciation, and a fall in the exchange rate an appreciation, we may conclude: the exchange rate for the country with the higher rate of inflation will depreciate; for in this case the difference between p and p^* will be (strictly) positive.

Let us furthermore introduce the real exchange rate, to be called Q, which is the nominal exchange rate S after dividing out by the price levels. And let us call q the (natural) logarithm of the real exchange rate. We then have:

$$Q \equiv S \cdot \frac{P^*}{P} \tag{3.6a}$$

$$q \equiv s + \ln P^* - \ln P \tag{3.6b}$$

$$\Delta_t q \equiv \Delta_t s - \Delta_t p \tag{3.6c}$$

Thus, if absolute purchasing power parity holds, by (3.3) and (3.6a) equation (3.7a) below will hold true, and by (3.4) and (3.6b) equation (3.7b) will hold true, while with relative purchasing power parity, equation (3.7c) will hold true by (3.5) and (3.6c):

$$Q = 1 \tag{3.7a}$$

$$q = 0 \tag{3.7b}$$

$$\Delta_t q = 0 \tag{3.7c}$$

Both absolute and relative purchasing power parity describe a goods market equilibrium, the equilibrium (due to arbitrage transactions) for buying tradeables. So PPP is a flow equilibrium, an equilibrium for the flow of currently traded commodities, an equilibrium on current account. The approach taken in this treatise, however, is an asset or stock approach. If 98 per cent or more of all foreign exchange transactions are not on current, but much rather on capital account an asset approach is the only sensible one. It is not sufficiently discussed in the literature how in this case purchasing power parity can be of any significance at all. The answer is two-fold.

One: even if exchange rates are determined solely on capital account, purchasing power parity may still hold. But in that case prices have to adjust to the (nearly) exogenously given exchange rate. This will be especially true for the case of relatively small nations or, more precisely, for currency areas in which international goods market transactions are a large percentage of all goods market transactions. For, in this case, the influence of externally determined prices on all prices will be strong. As pointed out already, purchasing power parity theory need not be an exchange theory at all; it may be just a theory of price determination, of prices internal to the economy.

Two: in general, investors will not necessarily want to invest in one country all the time. And they will normally be interested in the periodic return of their investment (in their interest or dividend income) in terms of its purchasing power at their main place of residence. For the first-named reason they will be interested in the purchasing power of the value of their foreign investment at some moment (as yet unknown to them) in the future when, for some reason, they will wish to repatriate the capital sum of their investment. And second, they are interested, period after period, in the purchasing power at home of their investment income.

In formulating the asset-analytic purchasing power parity problem, one has to take care not to confuse it with the problem of the rate of investment return in a foreign market. Any questions of changing asset prices over time in the foreign market as well as questions of the time change of interest, dividends, etc. in the foreign market belong to the latter theoretical domain. Or, to put it differently: purchasing power is the analysis of the price for the purchaser. A rising price level in foreign (equation 3.4) or, equivalently, a higher inflation in foreign (equation 3.5), is 'bad' for the buyer in foreign: she has to pay more and can buy less. This, therefore, tends to depreciate the foreign currency or, equivalently, to appreciate the home currency relative to foreign: S and s fall. If, however, an inhabitant of the home currency area buys a foreign asset and the price of this asset rises, this is 'good' for her: she can sell this asset and with the price received can, *ceteris paribus*, buy more in either foreign or home. As such, this resale perspective is alien to purchasing power parity. But if we want to analyse the asset holder's perspective of purchasing power parity, we must introduce at least a certain residual of a resale, and that would be the retransfer of one unit of the foreign currency (which as such does not change, i.e. is of a zero rate of return) at a future time point T back into home currency. At time 0 we receive one such unit of foreign currency for a price S_0 and, if need be, at time T we receive back S_T units of home currency.

Let us now introduce a probability to sell a foreign asset because of home need (liquidity problems at home, retirement need, death of the original investor, etc.). Let us call this probability π_T for time point T. Then the expected value V of a sum S_0 used at time 0 to purchase 1 unit of the foreign currency after repatriation and weighted with the probability of repatriation will be (writing S_t^e for the expected exchange rate at time t):

$$V = \sum_{t=1}^{\infty} \pi_t S_t^e \tag{3.8}$$

If purchasing power parity is expected to hold for all future periods and the price levels of home and foreign, to be called P_T and $P_T{}^*$, are correctly foreseen for each and every time point T, with time t running from 1 to infinity, we would have:

$$V = \sum_{t=1}^{\infty} \pi_t \frac{P_t}{P_t^*} \tag{3.9a}$$

A similar expression, though with other weights (and weights to be interpreted differently), could be formed for the purchasing power of current investment returns on foreign assets.

As equation (3.9a) is a sum, there can be no exact equivalent in logarithmic form from which to derive an equation equivalent to (3.5) for relative purchasing power parity. But, calling $\Delta_t s_t^e$ the expected logarithmic exchange rate change at present and $\Delta_t p_t^e$ the expected inflation differential at time *t*, we can – for the asset approach – write approximately:

$$\Delta_t s_0^e = \sum_{t=1}^{\infty} \pi_t \Delta_t P_t^e \tag{3.9b}$$

The important point of this discussion is: from the perspective of an investor in foreign, the expected exchange rate change according to relative purchasing power parity does not depend on present inflation differentials alone, but on a weighted sum of all future inflation differentials. This goes quite a way to explain the weak and slow mean reverting trend of exchange rates to PPP: partly, it reflects the complicated process of learning about likely future inflation differentials, and not only the probably much more rapid adjustment process of prices.

Of course, if interlocal inflation differentials follow a martingale over time, then the best forecast of future inflation differentials is the present interlocal inflation differential. Even for the asset approach of the investor, equation (3.9b) then collapses into equation (3.5). Then, and only then, nothing but current inflation differentials count. But such an assumption is implausible. Inflation differentials do depend on monetary policy; and policy is not totally unpredictable over time. In particular, with well-known presidents and boards of directors of central banks, one can normally form some longer-run expectations of the future monetary policy they are likely to follow. Thus, from the perspective of asset holders, who nowadays dominate exchange rate market transactions, standard PPP analysis is off the mark, because it looks only at current relative commodity prices.

At certain times, though, there are marked changes in monetary policy. For these, the present rate of inflation can be an important signal for future price developments to be expected. This would mean, however, that the coefficient of present inflation can, in an asset approach, deviate considerably from unity: if there is adaptive learning it would tend to be below unity. If a high present rate of inflation is a signal of accelerating inflation, and vice versa, the coefficient of the present inflation differential could exceed unity. Signalling effects may also mean that the time change of the interlocal inflation differential could serve as a supplementary relevant explanatory variable.

I have not discussed the numerous measurement problems in order to find appropriate price levels for an empirical application of PPP. Even so, considering the problems already pointed out, it is no wonder that MacDonald and Stein conclude: 'PPP is a poor guide to policy.'[5] This is an important factual conclusion from the experience of the floating rate era. For it was precisely as a measuring rod for policy conclusions that, following the lead of Gustav Cassel in the early 1920s, PPP had mainly been used.

Uncovered interest parity

Uncovered interest parity is the second equilibrium theory of exchange rates. With it we turn to the asset approach pure and simple. This is of foremost topical interest in the present world, where 98 per cent of all foreign exchange transactions are on capital account.

The economic logic behind uncovered interest parity is as simple and as fully convincing to professional economists as that behind purchasing power parity: the investment market, or the capital account between two currency areas, will only be in equilibrium if, after adjusting for differential risks, investors receive the same rate of return in both markets; and that must be the case – pairwise – for all capital markets. So if one market offers a higher return than another in local currency units, this advantage has to be taken away again by expected changes of exchange rates: the currency of the country with the higher rate of return has to depreciate just so much that the return differential is equalized. Let us take the rate of return in a currency area to be equal to 'the' interest rate (whose exact specification we shall discuss later). Let this nominal rate of interest for *one* period be called R for home and R^* for foreign, the exchange rate S_0 and the expected future exchange rate one period ahead S_1^e. Let us furthermore assume that there are no risk premia, i.e. investors are risk neutral. Uncovered interest parity then says:

$$(1+R)=(1+R^*)\cdot\left(\frac{S_1^e}{S_0}\right) \qquad (3.10)$$

This has to be so, for if we invest one unit of local currency at home for one period, at the end of this period we will have $1+R$ units, where the interest rate R is contractually fixed at time 0 and therefore a certain and precisely known rate of return. Thus, the left side of equation (3.10) is the return to investment in home. But if we transfer one unit of local currency to the foreign capital market, we do that at the spot exchange rate, S_0, and receive $1/S_0$ units of foreign currency. This we invest for one period in foreign at the interest rate R^*, which is contractually fixed at time 0 and therefore a certain and precisely known rate of return. If we reconvert our certain return at the end of period 1 to the home currency, we have to do it at the future expected exchange rate, S_1^e. Thus, the right-hand side of equation (3.10) is the expected return to investment in foreign. As investors are taken to be risk neutral, the certainty equivalent of the expected return is just the expectation value so that S_1^e can be interpreted as $E(S_1)$ or its mean expected value, the other quantities being nonstochastic known quantities anyway. For the capital market to be in equilibrium, the two rates of return have to be equal in expectation, the left side of equation (3.10) has to equal the right side and (3.10) has to hold.

Note that we cannot really use an arbitrage argument to derive uncovered interest parity: as the equivalence of equation (3.10) depends upon an expected future exchange rate for reconversion of foreign returns, the whole transaction is risky. We describe a speculative venture. That is the reason why the parity is called 'uncovered'. Only if expectations are quite correct and the expected exchange rate exactly equals the spot rate realized one period later, do we have:

$$(1+R)=(1+R^*)\cdot\frac{S_1}{S_0} \tag{3.10a}$$

Let us now take logarithms of the exchange rates, calling $\ln S_1^e/S_0 \equiv \Delta_t^e s$ and assume that $\ln(1+R)$ and $\ln(1+R^*)$ equal R and R^* respectively, which is, of course, approximately correct only for small values of interest rates. Calling, furthermore, $R-R^* \equiv \Delta_l R$ we get the basic equation:

$$\Delta_t^e s = \Delta_l R \tag{3.11}$$

The expected one period change in the log exchange rate (i.e. for small changes in the percentage change of the exchange rate) equals the interest differential between the two currencies. Note that once more the coefficient of ΔR in equation (3.11) is necessarily unity and positive.

It is easy to introduce risk premia for the case of non-risk-neutral investors. Let us call ρ the risk premium of home and ρ* the risk premium of foreign; and let us, as usual, call the difference of the risk premia Δ_l, thus: $\Delta_l\rho \equiv \rho - \rho^*$. Furthermore, let us define risk-adjusted interest rates as R' and $R^{*\prime}$ respectively, so that: $R' \equiv R - \rho$, $R^{*\prime} \equiv R^* - \rho^*$: and finally their difference $\Delta_l R' = R' - R^{*\prime}$.

Then we can modify equation (3.11) to:

$$\Delta_t^e s = \Delta_l R - \Delta_l \rho = \Delta_l R' \tag{3.12}$$

The expected one-period change in the log exchange rate equals the interest differential between two currencies after taking risk premia into account.

It is important to remember the following five points.

One: equilibrium here means *no* capital movements between different currency areas. Basically, it is assumed that financial market prices move instantaneously in order to reach the new equilibrium and therefore make capital movements unnecessary, even pointless. This notion derives from the idea of Keynes in the *General Theory* that financial market prices move very rapidly. But in his case a given stock of long-term bonds (or, on the other hand, money) is considered, which has always to be held by someone. In the case of world capital markets there is, however, a considerable volume of new capital constantly being created which has to be allocated to different currency areas, and not necessarily to those where this new capital originally came from. So we have very substantial capital flows the world over, and not least a very large capital inflow into the USA for every single year since 1982, that is, by now, for the last twenty years. This flow comes above all from Japan and Europe which are lender currency areas. Therefore, world capital markets are *not* in equilibrium in the sense of uncovered interest parity. Equations (3.10) to (3.12) thus cannot hold empirically. We shall also find a number of reasons why price adjustment, even on capital markets or on asset account, may be quite slow. Instantaneous adjustment is not a feature of international capital markets.

Two: the usual interpretation of the uncovered interest parity equation (3.10) assumes that the two interest rates, R and R^*, are given magnitudes, given especially by monetary policy and perhaps also by real magnitudes, by time and risk preferences as well as technology. Frequently a given monetary policy shock is assumed, which changes the interest rate only in the country where this policy shock occurs. These given interest rates then cause a change in the spot rate S_0. Thus, equation (3.11) is to be read in a *causal* sense from right to left, i.e. the right-hand side causes the left-hand side.

Another interpretation considers changes in the expected future exchange rate, S_1^e, in particular because of inflationary expectations, to which the present spot exchange rate, S_0, adjusts.

But these interpretations are not at all necessary consequences of the equilibrium story. They cannot even be justified by the relative adjustment speeds, alleged by standard theory: both interest rates and exchange rates are financial market prices, which 'should' both adjust instantaneously.

Actually, the rationale of the unidirectional effect of R on S is probably an implicit and by now outdated assumption about the US-American economy: As the exchange rate in the USA affects so 'few' prices because the economy has only a very small import and export sector (an assumption by now less and less valid, even for the USA), while the local interest rate affects very many prices, interest changes, conditioned by the home economy alone, have to cause exchange rate changes.

Perhaps this is still empirically correct for the USA. But for financially less dominant countries and for internationally more integrated countries it may very well be that changes in the foreign rate of interest cause above all changes of the home rate of interest, or partly such changes and only residually changes of the exchange rate. Also, changes in the spot exchange rate may very well cause changes in the rates of interest. German experience shows that changes in the US-dollar–German Mark exchange rate 'Granger-caused' changes both in the nominal and, of course – because inflationary changes were small in the real long-term interest rate.[6] Complex interactions between the variables in equation (3.10) do not contradict uncovered interest parity at all, which only says that in order for there not to be any capital flows (i.e. in order to remain in 'equilibrium' after a change) there should be some adjustment between the many variables in equation (3.10) in order to satisfy this equilibrium condition.

An even stronger statement may possibly be made as regards the case of Canada relative to the USA. It seems that the capital markets there assume that the two financial systems are so closely linked that interest differentials will soon be adjusted by capital flows to or from Canada. In such a case the exchange rate cannot be explained by uncovered interest parity at all, but simply moves erratically or in a way to be explained by other variables. Note that if it is assumed in expectations that the exchange rate shows martingale behaviour, that is, that the best forecast for the future exchange rate is the present one, then exchange rates drop out of equations (3.10) to (3.12) altogether; interest rates then differ only by a white noise term and, possibly, also a risk premium. Because of such interest rate expectations, the exchange rate regime behaves not unlike a fixed exchange rate regime in spite of the fact that it actually moves considerably. Of course, such direct interest adjustment holds even more strictly if the exchange rate actually is fixed.

Three: what is 'the' rate of interest in the two 'countries'? By stating equation (3.12) we have already pointed out that it may actually be a quantity which is unmeasurable directly, because 'the' rate of interest may have to be adjusted due to risk premia. In going somewhat deeper it is easy to realize that 'the' rate of interest for a given country is actually a complicated aggregate.

By the logic of the argument behind equation (3.10) it is actually a weighted average of various kinds of investment returns, weighted by the shares of the various investments in the investment portfolio of international investors. Originally one thought of international investors as holding only short-term instruments, commercial paper, for example, or treasury bills. In this view it would be the short-term interest rates, let us say the three months rate, if not even the money market rate that are relevant. But already in the classical gold standard era investors eagerly bought long-term bonds, i.e. government bonds and utility and transport bonds, for example, railway bonds.[7] Then it would be five year, ten year or thirty year bonds and their interest rates which are relevant. And if investors happened to shift their preferences between short and long-term bonds this would leave the difference of the aggregates in equation (3.11) unaffected only if the yield curves in the two currency areas showed equal differences between their short and long rates, or, to put it figuratively: if yield curves were 'parallel' to each other. This is a most unlikely condition to be fulfilled in practice.

Furthermore, in 1999 international investors seemed to have invested particularly on the US stock market. So 'the' relevant rate of interest would actually be the return on shares, which, of course, is not only the dividend return, but in addition also the change in stock prices. In the first half of 1999 the dominant 'interest' rate which appreciated the US-dollar and depreciated the euro was possibly this stock market return, expressed above all in an appreciation of the Dow-Jones and later the NASDAQ indexes. It not only appreciated the dollar, but also pushed up German interest rates by some one and a half per cent in the first half of 1999. Or, should we much rather say it was the boom in the NIKEI-index which appreciated the yen?[8]

All these are interest parity effects on the exchange rate (and other interest rates), rightly understood. But what if the investors are interested in direct investment or in buying real estate? Then, of course, their rates of return are the relevant 'interest' rate. To put it in a nutshell: 'the' rate of interest is really a *complex of many different rates of return* to financial investment, very difficult to measure and hard even to guess at. Over and above that, the aggregate is likely to be one of shifting weights: even if every single return differential between the two currencies remained the same if and when investors shifted on average to some other type of international investment, it would have just the same effect as a change in 'the' rate of interest. All this implies that even if uncovered interest parity were fully to hold at all times, measured interest parity would not be likely to hold empirically, for over time, the average investor uses different types of interest rates in their decisions.

Four: of course, it would be the rate of return after taxes which would count. In the light of interest parity, a change in the tax rate for the return on investment while the pre-tax return stays constant is just the same as if that rate of return had changed. An additional tax in home has just the same effect, as if home had lowered its interest rate; and conversely for foreign. Unfortunately, however, the burden of the taxes actually paid by foreign investors is notoriously difficult to estimate.

Hans-Werner Sinn has argued persuasively[9] that at least the latter part of the US-dollar appreciation by about 100 per cent relative to the German Mark from 1979 to early 1985 was due to the first Reagan tax reform of 1981. This reform had introduced substantial investment allowances for tax purposes and a kind of accelerated depreciation. Thus, the relevant investor, as seen by Sinn, was the one who was interested in direct investment: in order to profit from these tax allowances, funds had to be shifted to the USA and invested in the relevant kinds of real capital – and, according to Sinn's calculations, there ensued a very large volume of investment. On the other hand, the internationally more influential second Reagan tax reform of 1986, the enactment of which became more or less certain already in early 1985, lowered marginal tax rates all round. In order to do this it broadened the tax base and, in particular, took away the tax allowances for investment; it also lengthened the period of the allowable write-off of investment. According to Sinn this had the effect of causing the plunge in the dollar from early 1985 until 1987, a plunge approximately back to the 1979 exchange rate of the US-dollar against the German Mark. This appears to be a very plausible but much neglected story of the dollar movement, neglected by those who seek reasons for price shifts only in market reactions, without looking at the effects of government regulations.

Notice that, according to Sinn, the depreciation of 1985 to 1987 is not just the reaction of the exchange rate to the initial appreciation as it would occur according to interest parity where the country with the higher rate of return shows first an appreciation, to be followed by a depreciation: it would much rather be due to a tax policy change. Note, however, that it is quite difficult to explain why the appreciation lasted more than five years and even the depreciation lasted two. But that is a problem we shall return to later.

Five: if investors are interested in long-term financial investment, then the rates of return in equations (3.10), (3.10a) and (3.11) are not necessarily known and given: the relevant rates of return may be expected returns over a longer period, just as much expected values as the future expected exchange rate. In the stock market one has to estimate the likely rise of stock prices over time in order to calculate a rate of return. And Hans Werner Sinn's direct investors had to estimate how long the investment tax allowances would hold. In particular, in most kinds of long-term investment, a buy-and-hold strategy is usually more profitable than a series of short-term investments. Thus many relevant rates of return actually cannot be taken as being known with certainty at the moment of a shift of funds from one currency to the other.

The contradiction between purchasing power parity and uncovered interest parity

Just as with purchasing power parity, uncovered interest parity may be expressed in terms of real exchange rates.

Recall equation (3.6c) which is:

$$\Delta_t q \equiv \Delta_t s - \Delta_t p \qquad (3.6c)$$

Introduce the real rate of interest, to be called r for home and r^* for foreign. This is defined as follows:

$$r \equiv R - p \qquad (3.13a)$$

$$r^* \equiv R^* - p^* \tag{3.13b}$$

$$\Delta_l r \equiv \Delta_l R - \Delta_l p \tag{3.13c}$$

All these equations may also be written in terms of expectations, of course. For in intertemporal equilibria it is the expectations that matter. Thus, we can write equation (3.6c) in expectational form:

$$\Delta_t^e q \equiv \Delta_t^e s - \Delta_l p \tag{3.14}$$

If we use equation (3.11) and substitute equations (3.14) and (3.13c) into it, we get:

$$\Delta_t^e s = \Delta_t^e q + \Delta_l p = \Delta_l R = \Delta_l r + \Delta_l p \tag{3.15}$$

By deleting $\Delta_l p$ on both sides, we get:

$$\Delta_t^e q = \Delta_l r \tag{3.16}$$

We get exactly the same expression for uncovered interest parity in the real exchange rate which we had for nominal exchange rates: the expected one period percentage change in the real exchange rate equals the real interest differential between the two currencies.

Notice that if in equation (3.14) as well as in equation (3.13c) we had taken the differential in expected and not in actual rates of inflation, i.e. $\Delta_l^e p$ instead of $\Delta_l p$, we would have derived exactly the same equation (3.16), as the inflation term, if it is the same in an expression similar to equations (3.14) and equations (3.13c), just drops out. Thus we could also derive equation (3.16) from:

$$\Delta_t^e q = \Delta_t^e s - \Delta_l^e p \tag{3.17a}$$

$$\Delta_l r = \Delta_l R - \Delta_l^e p \tag{3.17b}$$

In fact, if the rate of inflation follows a martingale over time, then $\Delta_l p$, the actual inflation differential, is the best estimator for $\Delta_l^e p$, the expected inflation differential, for the next period in the future; and if subperiods are very short and we merge them together we can say that actual present inflation is a good estimator of expected future inflation. In this case, then, the two ways of looking at inflation do not differ.

It is common practice, however, to introduce the transformation of the nominal to the real interest rate via the Fisher equation. As is well known, the Fisher equation says that, in financial market equilibrium, the nominal rate of interest is the real rate of interest plus the expected rate of inflation; and that therefore, if the real rate of interest remains the same, the nominal rate of interest varies just with the expected changes in the rate of inflation. (As the rate of interest is a financial market price, this adaptation to inflation should, according to standard theory, happen very rapidly, just as the exchange rate should adjust very rapidly.) We do not have to write down the Fisher equation because, after taking regional differentials between two currency areas, it is just equation (3.17b) rearranged. But we actually do not need the idea behind the Fisher equation at all because, as argued above, equation (3.16) is derived just the same whether we take actual or expected rates of inflation on both sides. And in case the rate of inflation follows a martingale over time, the equivalence of actual and expected inflation may be argued, as pointed out above, independently of any equilibrium between debtors and creditors in the Fisher vein.

If we now gather equation (3.5) – with rational expectations – and equation (3.11) together we get equation (3.18), while if we gather equation (3.7c) – with rational expectations – and equation (3.16) together we get equation (3.19):

$$\Delta_t^e s = \Delta_l p = \Delta_l R \tag{3.18}$$

$$\Delta_t^e q = 0 = \Delta_l r \tag{3.19}$$

Remembering equation (3.13c), both equations (3.18) and (3.19) say the same as, of course, they have to by definition: the two equilibrium theories of exchange rate change, namely relative purchasing power parity and uncovered interest parity, can both hold true if and only if the real interest differential between the two currency areas is zero. Real interest has to be exactly the same in the two currency areas. And that constitutes in general a contradiction between the two theories explaining exactly the same expected one-period change in the exchange rate. The two equilibrium theories, which on the face of it are equally convincing, *cannot both hold true*!

This fact has been recognized in the literature, but is being glossed over. The standard textbook by Krugman and Obstfeld, for example, says: 'Expected real interest rates are [?] the same in different countries when relative PPP is expected to hold . . . More generally, however, expected real interest rates in different countries need not be equal, not even in the long run, if continuing change in output markets is expected.'[10] I see no reason why the first sentence should hold true. Much rather, PPP just takes no notice of interest rates, as the reader can verify by checking equations (3.5) and (3.7c).

It is only when we add uncovered interest parity that we realize we should make an additional assumption when stating PPP. In asset equilibrium, PPP has to assume equal real interest rates (if investors are risk-neutral). The second sentence, however, is the rub of the matter: why should risk and time preferences and technologies in different countries make real interest rates equal?

The counter-argument, of course, is that international capital movements will make real interest rates equal. But this is much too simplistic a view. In fact, we should remember the well-known argument by Robert Lucas (1988) who asks: 'Why Doesn't Capital Flow from Rich to Poor Countries?'[11] The answer is that there is not only substitution between factors of production, but that there are also complementarities between them; and the complementary factors to real capital – human capital of engineers and skilled workers, organizational talent, entrepreneurship and innovatory capacity – are not as mobile internationally as financial capital. Both legal framework and financial market organization may also differ from country to country and can have an important impact on real interest rates; in other words: institutions matter. Furthermore, when countries have different real growth rates, would not that argue for different real interest rates, as many types of theories assume?

Next we have to recognize that there will be cyclical variations of real interest rates. Thus, both PPP and interest parity can hold true only if business cycles are completely synchronized between currency areas.

Perhaps even more important, the Fisher equation holds true to a varying degree between countries. Until a short while ago higher sustained rates of inflation meant lower real interest rates; though, possibly, this may no longer hold true and even the opposite may now be the case.[12] Anyhow, monetary policy can have a substantial effect on real interest rates during a considerably extended period. And in the vein of Martin Feldstein[13] we might argue in addition that tax systems in different countries tend, in effect, to treat inflation differently, so that real after-tax rates of return are changed in a differential way.

Manfred Neumann has pointed out that with exchange rate volatility and international differences in time preferences countries with relatively low time preferences will not only become creditor nations, but 'overinvest' in the sense that their marginal productivity of capital and thus their real interest rates will be relatively low.[14]

There is still another point: as I have argued above at length, the relevant rate of return in the uncovered interest parity equation is not one single interest rate, but a complex composite index. So even if all the single real rates of return were the same in the two countries, the real rate of return index would still differ if investors should prefer a different mix of investments. And why should they not desire to have a different investment mix in different 'countries', as differences in sectoral structures between economies are, as foreign trade theory argues, a powerful reason for and possibly also a consequence of commodity exchange?

Finally, should we not adduce exactly the same argument for differences in real interest rates as is used in stating that relative PPP is more likely to hold than absolute PPP? There the argument was that, with barriers to full arbitrage and therefore permanent differences in price levels, we might expect an unchanging difference in price levels in absolute terms, a 'constant' which, however, drops out if we calculate differences over time of the logarithm of price levels. Constant differences in real interest rates are for similar reasons also plausible, but not a constant difference of zero.

It can be shown empirically that there are considerable differences in real interest rates even between the largest and most developed OECD countries. In 2000, Japan had the lowest and the USA one of the highest real interest rates, the difference being a full $2\frac{1}{2}$ per cent. Part of this may be due to differential risk premia, as will be argued later. But it is difficult to believe that this is the only cause of real interest rate differentials. If it were so, however, we would have to add the assumption of equal risk preferences of investors in the two currency areas for the exchange equilibrium theories to hold true.

Notes

1 Black (1986), op. cit., p. 540, Lecture I, note 20.
2 Ibid.
3 Gottfried Haberler, *Der internationale Handel – Theorie der weltwirtschaftlichen Zusammenhänge sowie Darstellung und Analyse der Aussenhandelspolitik*, Berlin 1933, p. 32.
4 Ibid. p. 34.
5 Ronald MacDonald and Jerome L. Stein, 'Introduction: Equilibrium Exchange Rates', in: MacDonald and Stein (1999), op. cit., pp. 1–17, here p. 14, Lecture II, note 25.
6 See the literature discussed in Lecture II, notes 4 and 5.
7 See, e.g. Charles P. Kindleberger, *A Financial History of Western Europe*, London 1984.
8 Actually, US-American stock prices cannot significantly explain the dollar–Mark or the dollar–euro exchange rates throughout the recent past; Japanese stock market prices, however, have good explanatory power. See, e.g. Margit Hraschek, *Hatten die jüngsten Aktienkurssteigerungen Auswirkungen auf die Wechselkurse?*, Master's thesis, University of Vienna 2000. Japanese stock market price changes seem to be the best explanations of the deviations of the yen from its PPP-value relative to the German Mark.
9 Hans-Werner Sinn, *Capital Income Taxation and Resource Allocation*, Amsterdam 1987; the same: 'Why Taxes Matter: Reagan's Accelerated Cost Recovery System and the US Trade Deficit', *Economic Policy*, 1 (1995), 240–50.
10 Paul R. Krugman and Maurice Obstfeld, *International Economics – Theory and Policy*, Reading, MA etc., 5th edn, 2000, p. 428.
11 Robert Lucas, 'Why Doesn't Capital Flow from Rich to Poor Countries?', *American Economic Review*, Papers and Proceedings, 80 (1990), 92–6; and 'On the Mechanics of Economic Development', *Journal of Monetary Economics*, 22 (1988), 3–42. See also Paul M. Romer, 'Increasing Returns and Long-Run Growth', *Journal of Political Economy*, 94 (1986), 1002–37.
12 It is at least clear that nominal interest rates vary much more than exchange rates, while price indices vary less. MacDonald (1999a), op. cit., Lecture I, note 1, shows: 'Interest differentials are much more volatile than exchange rates' (p. 688). Thus, real exchange rates certainly do not stay constant.

13 Martin Feldstein, 'Inflation, Income Taxes and the Rate of Interest: A Theoretical Analysis', *American Economic Review*, 66 (1976), 809–20; and *Inflation, Tax Rules and Capital Formation*, Chicago–London 1983; and 'The Costs and Benefits of Going from Low Inflation to Price Stability' in: Christina D. Romer and David H. Romer (eds), *Reducing Inflation*, Chicago–London 1997, ch. 3, pp. 123–56.

14 Manfred Neumann, 'Real Effects of Exchange Rate Volatility', *Journal of International Money and Finance*, 14 (1995), 417–26.

Lecture IV Divergence

Process analysis of temporal exchange rate equilibria

A second look at uncovered interest parity

Curiously enough, such a well-known equilibrium theory as uncovered interest parity is quite often misinterpreted in econometric analysis. One should remember that it is a one-period model; and great care is needed when specifying precisely what happens at the end of that period and at its beginning. One-period models in economics are actually very tricky. Or, to put the same point in another way: uncovered interest parity is a difference equation, in continuous time a differential equation. And in solving differential equations one has to be careful to specify initial conditions, and not just forget them. Surprisingly, even such an obvious and elementary point needs to be emphasized.

What will happen, furthermore, if we wish to examine not only one interest change, but a whole series of them? It turns out that it is not at all a trivial exercise to convert uncovered interest parity into a sequential model of not one, but a succession of many interest rate 'shocks'.

In this chapter – and, in fact, in the whole text – attention will be focused on the interest parity condition of exchange rates because it provides the usual asset market explanation for their movements. As asset markets (or the capital account) now dominate exchange rate transactions, this is my preferred approach. In the first and the third part of this chapter it is therefore also assumed that the equilibrium condition(s) of uncovered interest parity hold, i.e. that international capital markets are in, and stay in, zero flow equilibrium.

Let us restate the interest parity condition, equation (3.10), and renumber it equation (4.1) in this lecture:

$$(1+R)=(1+R^*)\cdot\frac{S_1^{\,e}}{S_0} \qquad (4.1)$$

Let us call time point 0 the instance in which a new interest rate 'shock' or 'innovation' occurs. Let us assume that up to that moment a certain development of the exchange rate, due to the previous interest constellation, has taken place. Let us call the end point of this development time point

-1 and its beginning time point -2. Time point -1 is actually just the same moment in time as time point 0, only, as it were, a second earlier: it is the starting point just before the interest shock is announced, while 0 is the 'same' point in time after this announcement. Let us assume for simplicity's sake – it merely simplifies the argument without changing anything of importance – that in the time period from -2 to -1 there was asset market equilibrium and no change in the exchange rate, with everybody realizing that there would be no change. This would also imply that R and R^*, home and foreign interest rates, were equal. Thus:

$$(1+R_{-1}) = (1+R_{-1}{}^*)\cdot(S_{-1}/S_{-2}) \qquad R_{-1} = R_{-1}{}^*,\ S_{-1} = S_{-2} \tag{4.2}$$

Now we have a one period 'shock' to an interest rate. Let us assume, for example, that home interest rises *ceteris paribus*, that is, instead of $(1+R_{-1})$ the interest factor is now $(1+\Delta R)\cdot(1+R_{-1})$, the multiplicative term $(1+\Delta R)$ being the shock. Furthermore, and that is the central point, as uncovered interest parity is a one period model, after the end of the period all interest rates are to return to their levels previous to the shock and, because of this, the expected exchange rate returns to its starting point before the shock as well. (If we had not, for simplicity's sake, assumed no change during the period before the shock, the expected exchange rate would return to the level to which it would have developed without the shock.) Thus, in the case discussed $S_1{}^e = S_{-1}$; $S_1{}^e$ being the expected exchange rate at the end of 'the' (one) period after the shock.

We then have:

$$(1+\Delta R)(1+R_{-1}) = (1+R_{-1}{}^*)\cdot\frac{S_{-1}}{S_0} \tag{4.3}$$

or

$$\frac{S_0}{S_{-1}} = \frac{1}{1+\Delta R} \tag{4.4}$$

But S_{-1}, the expected end point of the exchange rate development, is also the starting point of the exchange rate one second before the interest change, in our case when the rise in the home rate is announced. So equation (4.4) gives the jump in the exchange rate in the very second the new interest rate is announced. It states the initial condition for the one-period process of change of the exchange rate following this 'news', as described by the interest parity condition. Let us take logarithms and call Δ_{-1} the instantaneous change from time point -1 to time point 0, actually a time difference of dimension zero. We get:

$$\Delta_{-1}s = -\Delta_t R \tag{4.5}$$

while the interest parity condition, to be restated here from equation (3.11), says:

$$\Delta_t s = \Delta_l R \qquad (4.6)$$

Note that equations (4.5) and (4.6) only differ by the opposite sign. Equation (4.5) in this example says: if the home interest rate rises, *ceteris paribus*, there has to be a jump appreciation of the home currency. In our one-period example this jump has to be in the opposite direction, but exactly as large as the integral over all the instantaneous depreciations during this one period will be. The exchange rate has to appreciate in order that the depreciation following it will carry it back, at the end of the period, to exactly the same point from which it started. Thus, equation (4.5) states the initial condition necessary in order that the time path of (4.6) may be realized in equilibrium over the whole process.

For many students of exchange rates, this important point is difficult to grasp: in theory an interest rate shock causes two opposite, but logically necessarily connected, movements of exchange rates in order to preserve capital market equilibrium. In our case it is an instantaneous appreciation, followed by a more or less protracted depreciation. But the ensuing difficulty in econometric studies is even greater: because of the opposite movements, it is unlikely that any linear econometric model will ever capture uncovered interest parity well. It cannot capture it because of the highly non-linear, as it were, see-saw, development. And that is the simple reason why uncovered interest parity usually does not show up in the – actually only too simple-minded – usual exchange rate equations estimated;[1] and why, if interest rates show up, they frequently have the 'wrong' sign.

Our next question has to be: what does the single 'period' of the uncovered interest parity model actually mean in real time? It is, of course, nothing but the period which a given interest rate shock is expected to last; it is the expectational period. Now assume we apply the model to a real-time analysis. This might be a forecasting model or the periodicity of the data in an econometric testing model. Take, for example, one quarter of a year as the real-time unit in our period analysis: there is no reason whatsoever why a given interest rate change in home or in foreign should be expected to last exactly one real-time quarter of a year. Assume that a certain expected change in one of the interest rates will last n periods of real time. (Note: it need not actually last that long; the model is one of expectational equilibrium. So far, it is the expected duration alone that matters.) Then equation (4.5) will be modified as follows to equation (4.7), with (4.6) still holding good:

$$\Delta_{-1} s = -n \cdot \Delta_l R \qquad (4.7)$$

Immediately, we derive the very obvious result (which, however, is not sufficiently stressed in the literature): the longer a given interest rate change is expected to last, the larger will the initial exchange rate jump in the direction opposite to the equilibrium development over time, shown by uncovered interest parity, have to be. This has to be so in order that, at the end of a once and for all 'innovation', the exchange rate is once more back to its initial level (see Figure 4.1). All of this is due to the simple logic of dynamic programming. Now with real interest rate changes, and I shall argue these are of particular importance, we could easily think of a permanent change in the rate of interest due, for example, to some permanent growth advantage. What would the jump be then? To answer this, let n go to infinity in equation (4.5a) and you immediately realize: even a minute change, which is assumed to last forever, in the rates of interest between currency areas necessitates an infinite jump in the exchange rate on announcement. Uncovered interest parity cannot handle infinitely long changes of rates of return, even if it is considered independently from purchasing power parity.

So we have now found two fundamental anomalies: first, purchasing power parity and uncovered interest parity cannot both hold, unless there

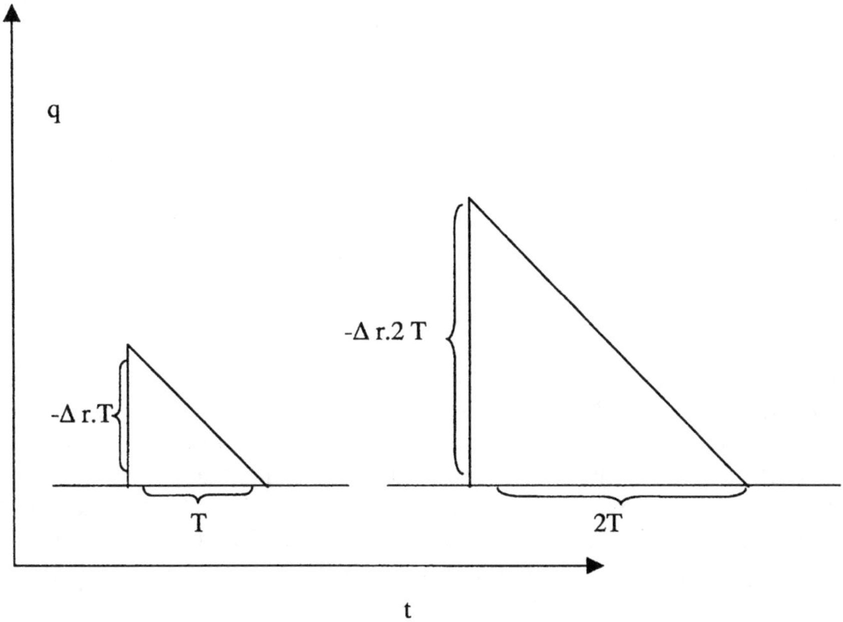

Figure 4.1 Change of the real exchange rate q after a change in relative interest rates expected to last for a short and for a long period.

Following a fall in the relative interest rate between two currency areas, the exchange rate in equilibrium 'jump-depreciates' followed by appreciation. The jump depends on the expected period of duration of the interest differential. If this period is twice as long as in the reference case, the initial jump has to be twice as large to preserve equilibrium.

is no difference in the level of real interest rates between the two currency areas. And second, uncovered interest parity by itself cannot handle a permanent change in the interest differential as an 'innovation' between the currency areas, as such changes would entail an infinite deplacement (an infinite jump) of the exchange rate variable.

These conclusions are somewhat surprising. For not only do the two equilibrium exchange rate theories explicitly and directly postulate empirically rather dubious equilibria – why should we call only a no-flow-of-capital-between-currency-areas case an 'equilibrium', when we constantly observe huge flows? Indirectly they postulate a third type of 'equilibrium', which is conceptually even more dubious: it only holds if real rates of returns between 'countries' are the same and in the long run always stay the same. If, as some who believe in (much too) rapid equilibration might do, we call a never changing world-wide equality of real interest rates 'international capital market equilibrium', we might then conclude that, according to the two equilibrium theories of exchange rates, exchange rates are in equilibrium. To me, this is rather a surfeit of equilibria – which can evidently tell us nothing about processes of change.

Note that the usual device of reducing long-term future effects to 'manageable' proportions and thus arguing them away, namely discounting them to the present, does not work here: the relevant discount rate of future exchange rates is exactly the interest differential, ΔR (and the discount factor $1 \cdot / \cdot 1 + \Delta R$). Thus, in discounted exchange rates the uncovered interest parity condition is exactly a martingale. Precisely because of that there has to be an infinite jump in case of a permanent change in the interest differential: the sum of all the discounted future changes in exchange rates does not converge. It grows beyond all bounds.

One way out would be to assume that the exchange market visualizes temporal changes of interest rate differentials as just random fluctuations around zero, towards which exchange rates need not adapt; and investors consider such interest fluctuations as too ephemeral to guide their investment decisions (which are to them mainly long-term decisions) and capital movements too costly to take advantage of such temporary investment opportunities. In this case, however, we have thrown out any explanation of exchange rates by interest rates altogether, and that is, perhaps, too radical a step, at least for some exchange rate regimes. But it may be a good explanation of the relationship between the Canadian dollar and the US-dollar: if two financial markets are very closely integrated, it is plausible that exchange rates should not react to interest rate shocks, because it is assumed that they will soon be ironed out, most likely by movements of capital. But exchange rates which do not react to interest rate changes may just as well be thought of as fixed in expectations. Then, as far as there is any price adjustment at all, and not only a quantity adjustment on capital markets, it will be Canadian interest rates that react to US interest rates and not the Canadian exchange rate, just as it would be with fixed exchange rates. Fixed exchange rate expectations might occur without fixed exchange rates. And such expectations would be rational.[2]

The most plausible alternative equilibrium explanation would be: interest rate changes are never expected to be permanent because nothing is permanent in this world. We might call this mean reverting interest expectations for the long run. In this case, however, the initial jump of the exchange rate (in the direction 'opposite' to the later movement) may still be large, if a long-run (though not infinitely long-run) change in the difference of interest rates is expected. Thus, it is not correct that we have to have recourse to the exchange rate overshooting model with sticky prices as an 'important phenomenon because it helps explain why exchange rates move so sharply from day to day', as the standard textbook by Krugman and Obstfeld[3] puts it. Simple uncovered interest parity with long-run expectations already explains that on its own.

Disequilibrium: slow quantity adjustment of capital

In the previous equations we used the uncovered interest parity equation, although we knew that huge capital flows were taking place between Germany and the USA, or at least the USA and other countries than Germany, such as Japan. Capital market equilibrium mostly did not exist. Can we still use something like the interest parity equation? The answer is: yes, we can – with modifications. But then we have to explain two things: first, when will there be a capital inflow or, conversely, an outflow? Second, why will the capital flows from country to country not be instantaneous, but slow?

The answer to the first question is, of course, that there will be a capital inflow if excess returns are to be earned in a given currency area. Calling *ER* the rate of excess returns at home and considering only a period with a constant interest differential ΔR, we will have:

$$ER = \Delta R - \frac{dS}{dt} \cdot \frac{1}{S} \tag{4.8}$$

If *ER* is positive we will have a capital inflow into home; if negative, an outflow. If we call dK/dt the amount of capital inflow in physical terms, i.e. capital inflow in terms of fixed international prices, the machines and raw material quantities transferred – note that this is not the relevant inflow in current account terms, because there a quantity of commodity inflow in fixed foreign currency prices has to be multiplied by the changing exchange rate – then it is plausible to assume:

$$dK/dt = f(ER) \qquad df/dER > 0 \tag{4.9}$$

Capital inflow is likely to be the larger, the higher the rate of excess returns. This would be the analogue to the well-known standard model of price adjustment in a supply and demand disequilibrium with linear supply and demand functions.

Now assume that there is a marked rise in the rate of interest in home, in particular a rise in the real rate. (The cases of a rise in foreign, or a fall in rates of return in home, would be analogous.) Assume that this rise is expected to last for a considerable length of time. Assume, furthermore, that after the initial shock the whole development is fully foreseen, that is, assume rational expectations. Then there are three possible cases.

One: qualitatively, much the same happens as in uncovered interest parity. Initially there is a jump appreciation of home's currency. But this is smaller than it would be if it were to choke off capital movements in the 'equilibrium' case of uncovered interest parity. After this the home currency depreciates, but less than would be the case in international capital market 'equilibrium': real capital in home cannot be built up sufficiently rapidly to cope fully with the new investment opportunities, which cause the rise in the rate of returns in home, so that foreign capital has to be attracted. In the typical Schumpeterian way the increase of the real rate of return in home is likely to decline, just as the additional investment opportunities decline. So depreciation is at a declining rate, as is capital inflow into home. Finally, rates of return are once more equalized internationally, capital inflow into home ceases, depreciation ceases and the exchange rate has once more returned to its initial value, just as it would do under uncovered interest parity.

Two: assume that the positive 'rate of return shock' in home is much larger than in the first case. For example: East Germany and East Central Europe open up to international commodity market and capital market integration in 1990; or South East Asia becomes fully integrated into the modern industrial world during the 1980s and early 1990s for the first time. Both of these cases are huge 'innovations' in the Schumpeterian sense, because Schumpeter includes, and I think rightly so, the opening up of 'new markets' as one of his five cases of innovation.[4] In both cases the real interest rate in home rises sharply, whether home is Germany or one of the South East Asian countries. If the capital markets in home and foreign are highly integrated, as may be the case with neighbouring countries that trade a lot with each other, the only effect could be that just the interest rate in foreign changes fully to the new interest level in home. This was more or less the case in France with respect to Germany in 1990 to 1992, because both had currencies closely linked in the European Currency System. It was partly the case in South East Asia in so far as currencies there were linked to the US-dollar. But it might also be the case between countries with floating exchange rates where the markets expect their movements to be mainly random with a zero mean difference, as in Canada with respect to the USA. In these cases interest rates would simply differ to the extent of the average marginal cost of shifting capital and there would be no or only negligible excess returns. But then there would also be, according to equation (4.9), small international movements of capital. If the rate of return shock is large and if the local rate of saving in home falls far below its desired rate of (real) investment, this small inflow of foreign capital will not suffice. A large capital inflow from foreign will typically cause excess demand for the currency of home at the given exchange rate. This will be so in particular with myopic expectations, but may also happen with long-term rational expectations which take the ensuing price change (the exchange rate movement) fully into account. Thus with a large increase in the rate of return at home we might easily get the apparently paradoxical situation that the home currency appreciates and that excess returns thus rise on both counts, both because of rising rates of return in home in local currency and because of continued exchange rate appreciation. Such very large excess returns may be necessary in order to attract foreign real capital sufficiently rapidly. By and by though, even such a large additional investment opportunity will exhaust itself. In Germany, for example, the investment boom lasted three years, from 1990 to 1992; in South East Asia much longer, a decade or more. With a declining real interest differential, appreciation will become less and finally peter out at the moment when interest rates are once more equalized and capital inflow stops. Thus we would have the following exchange rate movement: there may be some initial jump appreciation when the new innovational push is first realized. After that there will be a lengthy further appreciation over time, probably at a declining rate. At the end the exchange rate no longer changes because interest parity with equal rates of return is reached once more. But as there never needs to be a period of depreciation the exchange rate ends at a 'permanently' appreciated rate, due to this large shock of innovation, and because there never had to be a period of depreciation – 'permanently' here denoting: until reversed due to some other shock. Thus only the first part of interest parity holds true in this case: with higher rates of return at home there is appreciation 'at first', then declining appreciation during some time and never depreciation. As the new investment opportunities go hand-in-hand with a development of comparative advantages in international trade by the newly opened market, the final appreciation may also be in full accordance with long-run PPP, corresponding as it does to a permanent decline in real export prices.

Note, furthermore, that in this case, due to a continuous appreciation of the currency, foreigners enjoy higher rates of return than home investors during the whole period. Even in South East Asia with nominally fixed exchange rates (to the US-dollar), foreigners did enjoy higher returns than locals if they engaged or participated in direct investment, because a large investment boom tends to cause excess demand for other factors than capital and because the huge capital inflow from foreign cannot be fully sterilized by central banks so that the (nominal) stock of money rises and the price level will rise on both counts. But with rising price levels, the real exchange rate appreciates, even if the nominal one stays the same. Then, real returns are higher for foreigners than for locals. This higher return for foreigners has the effect of crowding out locals from the investment market. The investment boom as such already has the effect of throwing the balance on current account temporarily into deficit. The higher rate of return for foreigners is likely to reduce the rate of saving in home. This will increase the current account deficit even more. Most South East Asian countries as well as Germany from 1990 onwards rapidly developed a large current account deficit – for rate of return reasons, not for commodity price reasons, especially because foreigners enjoyed higher rates of return than locals. It is quite true what Boehm-Bawerk said in this respect: 'The balance of payments commands, the balance of trade obeys, not the other way around.'[5] But this asset account nexus tends to be forgotten today.

Three: the third case in parts resembles the second, but has a different ending. It is Hans-Werner Sinn's case of the introduction of large investment allowances in terms of taxes in a very large country, the USA in 1982.[6] In this case it is only after-tax returns and, as in the above case, only those on real investment that are increased. Otherwise, technical investment opportunities remain the same. In this basically stationary case in terms of investment opportunities and with a substitutive neoclassical production function in terms of capital or, equivalently, with a schedule of investment opportunities with higher and lower rates of return, the rate of interest after a tax-subsidy-induced investment boom has to be lower. The investment boom will still take place, even if its temporary nature is realized in terms of rational expectations: the investment tax allowance causes after-tax interest rates to be 'front-loaded', while the subsequent lower interest rates, this 'back-loaded' lower series of rates, will be discounted and will thus count for less. At least, standard literature (for example, by Dale Jorgenson)[7] has found that tax allowances will cause a positive investment reaction, even if interest rates drop over time due to increased investment. In this case then we might get jump appreciation upon the introduction of the tax favours, further continuous appreciation, probably at a declining rate during the time of capital inflow, but *at the end* of that, in 'equilibrium', further current appreciation, after the investment allowance ends in a possibly perfectly foreseen way. This is so because the rate of interest in home has now fallen below that in foreign and – in capital market equilibrium – this has to be evened out, due to interest parity, by constant appreciation. So in Sinn's case we have permanent, unending appreciation. The depreciation of the dollar from 1985 to 1987 was not part of that tax scenario, but, as Sinn rightly remarked, of another scenario following it. And just as in the second case studied here, a current account deficit results during the tax boom because foreigners receive higher returns than the locals.

Let us summarize: outside of capital market 'equilibrium' (and we hardly ever seem to be in it) even for the three great currency blocks – the USA, Euro-Europe and Japan – with their large capital movements, exchange rates may move away from a former equilibrium and, after 'equilibrium' has been regained, stay at the altered level once reached; or even diverge further. Uncovered interest parity postulates an equilibrium for exchange rate change, but not for the exchange rate level; and in its equilibrium, change can proceed wherever the level of the exchange rate finds itself. We have also realized that the initial impact, for example, an initial appreciation in case of a rise in the home interest rate, may be protracted and that an ensuing counter-change of depreciation may never occur. All this was true already for the case of each individual agent acting rationally, in private value terms, without looking at what the others do. In the case of herd behaviour, that is, if everybody is only interested in resale values by considering 'what average opinion expects the average opinion to be', all this will be further aggravated.

Let us now turn to the answer to our second question: why should capital movements be expected to be slow? For only if they are slow can there be protracted periods of capital market 'disequilibrium' in the sense of international capital flows, the case examined above.

Flows of financial capital are linked to investment in real capital; for, frequently, they are just the finance side making real investment feasible. That real investment takes considerable time to be effected after certain data important for determining the desired capital stock have shifted was extensively discussed in the 1950s. First, a sufficient number of agents have to realize that the data have actually changed. Then new lines of production and consequently new investments have to be planned. Two questions have to be answered: what is to be produced, and what is the best kind of capital equipment to produce? When this has been decided, one will often find that producers of investment goods do not have sufficient stocks or even sufficient capacity to satisfy investment demand immediately; and so on. All this entails lengthy periods of demand for new means of financing, the expansion of real capital and consequently lengthy periods of international capital movements both in commodity terms and in financial means. It has been fully realized in the optimum-growth literature that it takes time until a new equilibrium of capital stock is reached. Why this fact has mostly been ignored in the standard exchange rate literature is difficult to explain.

We now turn to purely financial capital movements, for example, buying foreign stocks and bonds. Ignoring long drawn-out capital adjustments in such a case of pure financial capital movement is probably due to the highly influential vision of Keynes, as embodied in the *General Theory*. In order to stress the importance of the asset approach to financial markets, Keynes frequently made his point by implicitly assuming that there was only a given stock of assets, which remained unchanged. This was more realistic for his times than for ours, namely for the 1930s, when there was little real investment and little issuance of new shares and additional bonds. But the fact that, commonly, the stock of assets is large, relative to the flow of new assets, and therefore very important, does not mean that the latter never counts. And second, and once more appropriate to his times, Keynes had a basically competitive theory of financial markets: when preferences or expectations change, prices change immediately. But present international financial markets are competitive, as one might say, in the small, but not in the large, in the case of large movements of capital.[8]

Today's international financial markets are dominated by so-called large 'players', by huge pension and investment funds and, not least, by governments. What happens if, for example, a large US investment fund gets fed up with so much 'home bias' in its portfolio and decides to switch a substantial portion of its portfolio to Japanese stocks? It can do so easily by reinvesting its current interest and dividend flow in Japanese stocks. But this would mean that funds are shifted rather slowly. If it wishes to switch its funds more radically, it will have to sell part of whatever funds it holds at the moment of the decision. But here the non-competitive element comes in: it will have to sell these funds very slowly in order not to ruin the price of its own assets. Only a small investor can sell out quickly without regard to the effect of her own sale on the price she achieves! After having sold its US funds slowly in order not to spoil the price to be attained, our investment fund will then have to shift its funds into yen, and once more it will have to operate slowly. What happened on October 6, 1998, when within a few hours the yen appreciated relative to the US-dollar by a full 15 per cent, just because a few investors wanted to shift from one financial market to another, may serve as a permanent warning to all those who wish to acquire foreign currency too rapidly. And on the Japanese side, bonds and stocks again will have to be bought slowly and in small quantities; for otherwise the price of these assets will be bid up disproportionately. The conclusion is: in financial markets dominated by large players, funds have to be shifted slowly and thus over a protracted period of time. As Genotte and Leland have shown, even hedging has to go on slowly, for otherwise it could be misinterpreted, as due to new 'fundamental' information, and bring on a mass stampede.[9]

Thus the build-up of real capital takes time and the reallocation of funds has to be achieved slowly, for otherwise what are basically transaction costs would explode. Transaction costs also explain why large changes in rates of return would make it more profitable to switch funds more rapidly and thereby increase the speed of capital flows. But there is also a third reason, developed above all by Karen K. Lewis: it will take time to find out whether a change in data has actually taken place.[10] This will be particularly true if a change in a rate of return in a certain currency area is due to the intertemporal price change of an asset which tends to fluctuate stochastically. Has the rise in US stock market prices finally petered out or has it even by now been permanently reversed? And is there really a rise in real returns due to the 'new economy'? Learning models are not yet fully developed in economics and are often still rather primitive. But it is common knowledge that learning takes time. The long drawn-out appreciation of the US-dollar against the euro in 1999 and 2000 was probably due to such a slow learning process, both as to returns in the USA and the likely policy of the European Central Bank. And it is quite unclear whether the correct conclusions have actually been drawn as yet.

A stochastic model of the development of the exchange rate over time

Let us now return to the two equilibrium theories of exchange rates, purchasing power parity and uncovered interest parity, and construct a fully articulated equilibrium model of exchange rate development over time, embodying both of these equilibrium theories. As we are interested in an asset-theoretic approach, we assume that uncovered interest parity always holds exactly, presumably because of instantaneous capital market adjustment to nascent disequilibrium. As to purchasing power parity, we shall assume that it holds on average. This is very much in the spirit of the usual equilibrium analysis where short-run deviations from PPP are always permitted. It is simpler to construct our model as one for the real exchange rate, whose logarithm is to be called q, as before. But this is an inessential simplification, as I intend to show. So our first assumption will be that the rate of inflation is perfectly known (or perfectly forecastable) to all market participants and that both exchange rates and interest rates always fully adjust to it in the usual way of PPP and the Fisher equation. Formulated in continuous time, PPP would be given by equation (4.10a), where we write $\hat{q}$ for the average of q to show that this need not be the value of q realized without exception in our system, and uncovered interest parity by equation (4.10b), where r, r^* are, as before, the real interest rates in home and foreign with $\Delta r \equiv r - r^*$:

$$\hat{q} = 0 \tag{4.10a}$$

$$\frac{dq}{dt} = \Delta r \tag{4.10b}$$

Now let us introduce real interest rate shocks over time. Assume that in the i-th period the real interest differential is Δr_i and that this differential will hold for a period of length T_i, which is exactly known to all market participants. If we then start out at time 0 at the PPP-equilibrium point, $q_0 = 0$, we get, by solving the differential equation (4.10b) and assuming as a terminal condition the return at time T_i to $q_{Ti} = 0$:

$$q_t = \Delta r_i(t - T_i), \qquad 0 \le t \le T_i \tag{4.11}$$

Next, we assume rational expectations or efficient financial markets. This implies a martingale for the real exchange rate, at least for the starting point of our process where we assume we start at $q_0 = 0$, i.e. at PPP-equilibrium. In order to get equilibria compatible according to both theories we know that we have to satisfy equation (4.12b) as well: the interest differential has to be zero on average. Introducing the expectation operator E we assume:

$$E(q) = 0 \tag{4.12a}$$

$$E(\Delta r) = 0 \tag{4.12b}$$

Thus, our process will describe the fluctuations, due to uncovered interest parity, of the log real exchange rate q around zero, which is its purchasing power parity value.

Now for the stochastic element in our model, implicitly already assumed when we introduced expectations in (4.12a) and (4.12b).

Let us assume that the interest shocks follow a stochastic process both as to their size and their timing. The size distribution of the interest differential shall have the following characteristics: Δr_i shall denote the i-th sample realization of a stochastic variable ρ denoting the amount of the interest shock. ρ shall be distributed in a symmetric, but otherwise quite general way around its mean zero. Each drawing from this distribution shall be independently distributed and have the identical distribution as all the others: ρ shall be an i.i.d. variable. And it shall also be independent of the theoretical time variable for the time of drawing, to be called τ.

$$E(\rho) = E(\Delta r_i) = 0 \tag{4.13a}$$

$$var(\rho) = \sigma^2{}_r \tag{4.13b}$$

For the time distribution of 'drawing' a new interest shock or innovation, with time variable τ, we shall assume a more specific distribution. But this specific nature is quite immaterial to our main results: we assume it only for the sake of clarity and in order to derive an explicit, closed-form solution. The distribution we choose is the most common distribution for the time of waiting between one occurrence and the next, in this case the waiting period between a given interest shock, Δr_i, and the next one, Δr_{i+1}. The shock Δr_i shall last exactly for a sample time period T_i, at the end of which the next shock will take place. If waiting times are independent and the probability of further waiting is always the same, whatever length of time one has waited already, the distribution in continuous time is the (negative) exponential distribution. Then the probability pr that τ takes the value x will be:

$$pr\tau(x) = 1/T \cdot e^{-x/T} \qquad x > 0 \tag{4.14}$$

The theoretical mean for τ and thus for the sample realizations T_i and its variance are given by equations (4.15a) and (4.15b):

$$E(\tau) = E(T_i) = T \tag{4.15a}$$

$$var(\tau) = T^2 \tag{4.15b}$$

Next we have to turn to the question of what market participants know. First of all, and typical for models of efficient financial markets, they know the precise time distribution of the interest shocks postulated above. Second, and typical for the standard interest parity model, they know each new interest differential precisely as to its magnitude and the moment it occurs: they know Δr_i. Third, they are, as is usually assumed, risk neutral – or, alternatively, the shock is already one after the deduction of the relevant risk premia. (Because of this they do not even have to know higher moments than the first of the size distribution of these interest shocks; that distribution is immaterial to them.) And fourth, and most importantly, at the moment when each new interest shock occurs it is announced how long it will last. That is to say: T_i, too, is common knowledge. Then we get the following process over time.

Starting from $q_0 = 0$, an interest shock Δr_i, lasting unchanged for a time period T_i, is announced. At this moment q jumps to $-\Delta r_i \cdot T_i$ (the initial condition of the interest parity process). Then, during the duration of this interest shock, q moves over time according to $dq/dt = \Delta r_i$. At the end of period T_i it has returned again exactly to $q = 0$. Then the whole process starts again with the next interest shock, Δr_{i+1} lasting for a period of length T_{i+1}. The time profile of the log of the real exchange rate, q, is saw-toothed with upward and downward 'teeth' of varying size and exactly corresponding length along the axis of $q = 0$ (see Figure 4.2). As these 'teeth' have

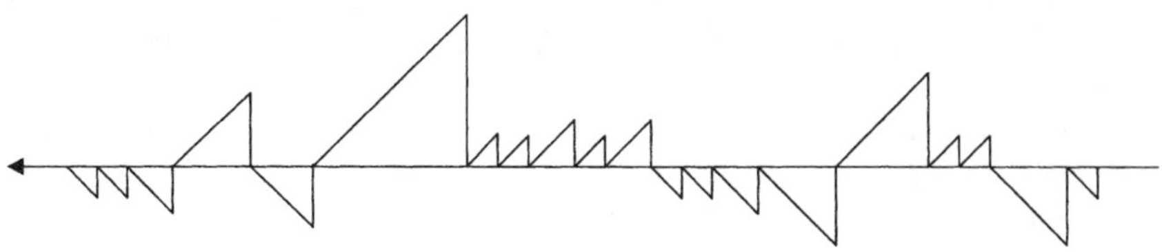

Figure 4.2 Interest parity with known duration of interest differentials.

Given certainty in the knowledge of the size and duration of each change in relative interest rates, the exchange rate fluctuates around a given trend.

triangular size distribution over time, the variance, *var*, over the whole process is exactly

$$var = 1/12\ \sigma^2_r \tag{4.16}$$

where σ^2_r is the variance of the size of the various interest differentials.

This variance is time-independent and constant. This is what most observers would expect such an equilibrium exchange rate process to look like. It is a 'natural' price process in the sense of Adam Smith with a 'central price', that is, $q = 0$, 'to which prices ... are continually gravitating'. Note, furthermore: although the forcing process, the process of the stochastically varying interest rate shocks at stochastic time intervals, has itself (as can easily be shown) a variance increasing linearly over time, the resulting exchange rate profile has constant, time-independent variance.

But that is only so because we have assumed that market participants know exactly the time duration of each new interest differential shock. That is a kind of knowledge of the future which strains all belief. We have already made very strong informational assumptions anyhow. The most that is still plausible is that we change assumption four above to assumption (*4′*): when a new interest shock Δr_i occurs market participants do not know what the exact time realization of that shock will be, but assume that it will last the average length for such shocks, T. So they know the time distribution of shocks, already a very strong informational assumption, but they do not know in advance its individual realizations.

Of course, the actual realization T_i will only with measure zero be exactly equal to the mean value, T. We now have the following process over time: when a new interest shock, Δr_i, is 'announced', q jumps from *wherever it is* by the amount $-\Delta r_i T$. It then develops, as before, according to $dq/dt = \Delta r_i$. But as this development ends after time T_i and not after T, the end point of the process in q-space is either lower or higher than the starting point, according to whether T_i is smaller or larger than T. The individual processes thus neither start necessarily at $q = 0$ (apart, by assumption, for the first process) nor do they end at it. But that should not matter much, one might assume, because, on average, the end points of the exchange rate development due to a given interest shock just fluctuate stochastically around their initial points. This conjecture is false. Now there is no price any longer 'to which prices ... are continually gravitating'.

It is easy to calculate the variance over time of the end points of the individual processes of exchange rates over time, which is exactly as in equation (4.17). Neglecting the change of the exchange rate between endpoints, which is, after all, only adding mean values between these various endpoints and therefore negligible for long periods with many interest shocks, we get as an approximate value of the variance of the whole process:

$$var(q) \sim T^2 \cdot \sigma^2_r \cdot t/T = T \cdot \sigma^2_r \cdot t \tag{4.17}$$

Equation (4.17) is derived as follows: during a total time period t for the process we have on average t/T interest shocks, as on average a shock lasts for a time T. As all the shocks are distributed independently of each other, both in size and in time, for a total length t of the process we have merely to add the t/T variances for the individual interest rate shocks. The variance of the size of the individual interest rate shocks is σ^2_r. As to the amount of the reduction (in absolute terms) of this initial shock, note that the time dimension of this reduction corresponds exactly one to one to the state dimension in q, because all the reaction triangles of uncovered interest parity after an initial jump are isosceles rectangular triangles in t and q, due to the coefficient of unity in equation (4.10a). The only thing we have still to prove then is that the variance of the incomplete or overcomplete build-downs of the initial jumps in q, due to a new interest shock, is T^2 per unit of this jump. This can be shown as follows.

The probability density function of the stochastic time variable is $1/T \cdot e^{-x/T}dx$ and runs from 0 to ∞. In the q dimension (the logarithm of the real exchange rate) the relevant variable is $z = T - x$, the exponentially distributed variable x subtracted from its mean T, because initially for $\Delta r = -1$ the q variable jumps for a mean expected duration of T by T and is then built down, one to one, over time for a period shorter or longer than T. The variable z has probability density function $1/T \cdot e^{\frac{z-T}{T}} dz$ and now runs from $-\infty$ to T, due to the transformation of the variable. As equation (4.18a) proves, this is again a probability density function which has, as equation (4.18b) shows, a theoretical mean of zero and, according to equation (4.18c), a variance of T^2:

$$\int_{-\infty}^{T} \frac{1}{T} e^{\frac{z-T}{T}} dz = 1 \tag{4.18a}$$

$$\int_{-\infty}^{T} z \cdot \frac{1}{T} \cdot e^{\frac{z-T}{T}} dz = 0 \tag{4.18b}$$

$$\int_{-\infty}^{T} z^2 \cdot \frac{1}{T} \cdot e^{\frac{z-T}{T}} dz - [0]^2 = T^2 \tag{4.18c}$$

The variance is the same then as that of the original waiting time distribution. The variance of the individual jumps of the logarithm of the real exchange rate is $T^2 \cdot \sigma^2_r$ and the total variance over time is $T^2 \cdot \sigma^2_r \cdot t$. Q.E.D.

What have we found? First of all, we have derived theoretically that taking both purchasing power parity and interest parity together the real exchange rate (and the same will be true of the nominal exchange rate) will essentially follow a random walk without drift. This is the first theoretical derivation in the literature, using the two equilibrium exchange rate

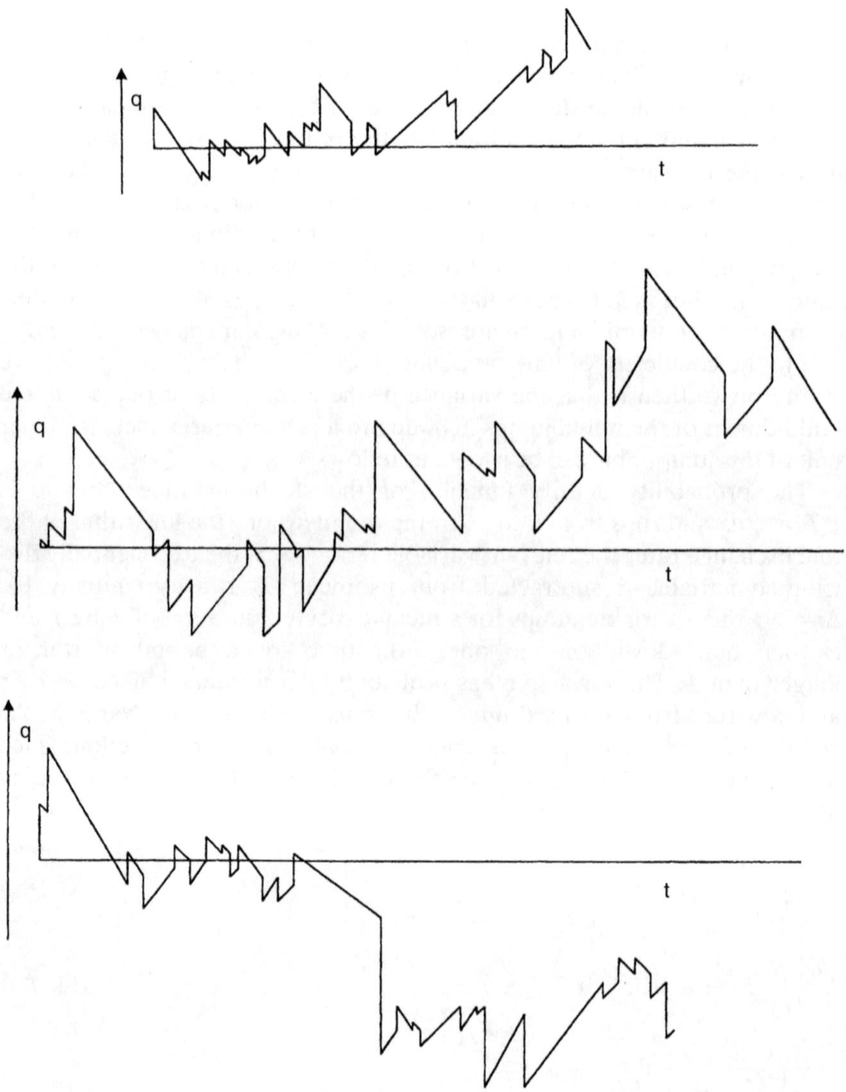

Figure 4.3 Interest parity with known average duration of relative interest rate shocks but unknown actual realizations of their time of duration.

Three randomly chosen simulations show the divergence from any long-run expected trend.

theories stated, of the point empirically demonstrated by Meese and Rogoff (1983). Basically, it uses only the idea that shocks to interest differentials follow a stochastic process over time whose mean duration alone is known to market participants.

Actually our process is more complicated than a strict random walk without drift: while the random walk has step length one (or zero), our 'step lengths', that is, the individual initial jumps, have an arbitrary symmetric distribution around zero; and while the time interval for the strict random walk is fixed once more at unity, we have a waiting time between jumps which is exponentially distributed. (Though it has to be pointed out once more that this distribution is, on the one hand, a plausible, commonly used waiting time distribution whose exact nature, on the other hand, is immaterial for our result.) But, as William Feller, who thoroughly studied the random walk without drift, has pointed out, these sophistications are actually not essential for the basic results:

> Under surprisingly mild conditions the nature of the individual changes is not important because the observable effects depend only on their expectation and variance. In such circumstances it is natural to take the simple random-walk model as a universal prototype.[11]

Our second conclusion is even more provoking, though a matter of course, once one has established the basically random walk nature of the double equilibrium exchange rate process: the variance of the logarithm of the real exchange – and, by extension, also the nominal exchange rate – increases proportionately with the length of time whenever the process starts from purchasing power parity. There is no mean reverting tendency whatsoever, no level towards which the exchange rate is 'constantly gravitating', simply because interest parity as such is without memory relative to past interest rate shocks and also completely unconcerned about purchasing power parity. The exchange rate is without anchor, exactly according to the standard equilibrium theories. It follows pure Schumpeterian innovation with unforecastable future results, apart from the fact that each innovation builds on the last one (the martingale effect that the best forecast for the future state is always the present state). This non-mean reverting nature, in fact, the diverting nature of the process, is empirically very plausible for the medium run: exchange rate variations since 1973, since the beginning of the new flexible exchange rate regime, have been huge. But, on the other hand, it has frequently been shown that trends in exchange rates shift and that periods of low and high variance alternate, but that over very long periods the variances of exchange rates around their trends remain constant. (Note that, by assumption, in our model the trend is always zero.) For the very long run then, our result is counterfactual. After first developing some further conclusions from the basic results derived at the end of this lecture, the main question in the next lecture will have to be: what may the long-run stabilizing effects to exchange rates be, after all? For, as our model has shown, large deviations from purchasing power parity are not at all surprising according to standard theory. An increasing variance of exchange rate movements is not surprising. What is surprising is much rather that, in the course of time, this variance does not pass all bounds.

Some further aspects of random walks

Let us return once more to the statement made above about the diffusion behaviour of the exchange rate if it follows both uncovered interest parity and purchasing power parity over time and state further mathematical results. William Feller (1967) was quoted there (see p.77).[12] Or, as Cox and Miller put it:[13] 'In general a diffusion process is determined, apart from boundary conditions, by its infinitesimal mean and variance respectively.' In our case the initial condition was simply that the exchange rate 'particle' starts at time zero at full equilibrium, a real exchange rate $q_0 = 0$, and that its process of development has mean zero, thus corresponding to a random walk without drift. As to such a driftless random walk, Cox and Miller point out:

> It follows from our results that, starting from state 0, the particle reaches any other given state with probability one, but that the mean time to achieve this passage is infinite. Having reached the given state it will return to state 0 with probability one, again with infinite mean passage time. Thus an unrestricted particle, if allowed sufficient time, is certain to make infinitely large excursions from its starting point and is also certain to return to its starting point.[14]

The economic consequence is that, for such an exchange rate process, there is no 'natural' price in the sense of Adam Smith: there is no 'central' price 'to which the prices ... are continually gravitating'. Furthermore, there can be no profitable speculation which is necessarily price-stabilizing in the sense of Friedman: for if stocks have time-variable costs, for example, interest costs, there can be no profitable stock holding if waiting time for a desired price is always infinitely long on average. And in the case of such a random walk without drift, one does not know whether a price is 'high' or 'low'.

Once the exchange rate is close to purchasing power parity in the model developed at the end of Lecture III, it tends to stay there, so that at times it looks as if an exchange rate stabilizing force were at work. But this tendency to stay close to PPP is merely due to the fact that in a random walk without drift the expected value is always that value where the 'particle' actually is. So the converse is also true: if the exchange rate is far away from purchasing power parity it tends to stay far away as well. In fact, Feller developed an *arc sine* law for the driftless random walk: states close to the mean, i.e. in our case purchasing power parity, are much less likely than values far away from it, in either direction. Furthermore, 'the average time between returns is bound to increase roughly linearly'.[15] Artificially generated driftless random walks, for example, by coin tossing, counting heads as plus one and tails as minus one, generate pictures with a wave-like pattern looking very much like empirical patterns of exchange rate behaviour. And it should be remembered that, in particular, the real exchange rate of many of the main currencies shows such slow mean reversion, if any, within the past dozen years or so that it cannot be statistically distinguished from a random walk (or, rather, martingale behaviour).

When conforming to this model then, exchange rates will show aimless fluctuations around purchasing power parity. The variance of the gyrations should increase over time. And note that the model presented has rational expectations embedded in it. The real puzzle, therefore, is not that more than a quarter century after the full introduction of flexible exchange rates in 1973 there is no sign that the exchange rates of the 'Great Three' currencies, US-dollar, German Mark (or its successor euro) and yen are coming significantly closer to their respective purchasing power parities. This was to be expected. The puzzle is rather that they do not diverge even further. True, there are periods when the variance of given exchange rates seems to increase. But then, once more, periods with lower variances follow. This has to be explained. So our question in the next two lectures will be: what are the stabilizing effects on exchange rates? Such forces have to come from outside those considered in a model using only two equilibrium conditions of exchange rates, purchasing power parity and interest parity. In particular, interest parity embodies no such equilibrating tendencies if the exchange rate is far away from purchasing power parity. Interest parity, being just a state-independent differential equation, is memoryless. The following lectures will be devoted to a search for other effects than purchasing power parity as such which might be stabilizing for the exchange rate variance and keep it roughly constant over time.

Notes

1 See, e.g. Marianne Baxter, 'Real Exchange Rates and Real Interest Rate Differentials: Have We Missed the Business Cycle Relationship?', *Journal of Monetary Economics*, 33 (1994), 5–37.

2 Jerome L. Stein, 'The Evolution of the Real Value of the US-Dollar Relative to the G7 Currencies', in MacDonald and Stein (1999), op. cit., pp. 67–101, Lecture II, note 25, comes close to modelling such a structure for some of his determinants of exchange rates: 'The crucial fundamentals $Z(t)$ are a stochastic process . . . such that there is no stationary distribution function, and uncertainty increases as one looks further into the future' (p. 73).

3 Paul R. Krugman and Maurice Obstfeld, *International Economics – Theory and Policy*, Reading, MA etc., 5th edn, 2000, p. 389.

4 Joseph A. Schumpeter, *The Theory of Economic Development* (R. Opie trans.) originally 1934, now New York 1961, p. 66, case (3).

5 Eugen Ritter Boehm von Bawerk, 'Unsere passive Handelsbilanz', op. cit., Lecture II, note 2, here p. 508 (my translation). Boehm makes it clear that he considers a change on capital account, a rise in international indebtedness to be the cause of the current account deficit. (In German this reads: 'Die Zahlungsbilanz befiehlt, die Handelsbilanz gehorcht, nicht umgekehrt.')

6 See Lecture III, note 9.

7 Robert E. Hall and Dale W. Jorgenson, 'Tax Policy and Investment Behavior', *American Economic Review*, 57 (1967), 391–414; Dale W. Jorgenson and Kun-Young Yun, *Tax Reform and the Cost of Capital*, Oxford 1991.

8 Note that error-adjustment models of an estimated exchange rate depending on long-run interest rates, with error adjustment depending on short-run interest rates (like the model of Ronald MacDonald and Mark P. Taylor, 'The Monetary Model of the Exchange Rate: Long Run Relationships, Short Run Dynamics and How to Beat a Random Walk', *Journal of International Money and Finance*, 13 (1994), 276–90, and its numerous successors) tend to assume that the adjustment of the exchange rate to capital market shocks is not instantaneous and thus that capital movements will ensue. For the error-adjustment assumption is difficult to rationalize with sticky commodity prices.

9 Gerard Genotte and Hayne Leland, 'Market Liquidity, Hedging, and Crashes', *American Economic Review*, 80 (1990), 999–1021.

10 Karen K. Lewis, 'Can Learning Affect Exchange Rate Behavior? The Case of the Dollar in the Early 1980s', *Journal of Monetary Economics*, 23 (1989), 79–100; and 'Puzzles in International Financial Markets' in: Gene M. Grossman and Kenneth Rogoff, *Handbook of International Economics*, vol. III, Amsterdam etc. 1995, ch. 37, pp. 1913–71.

11 William Feller, *An Introduction to Probability Theory and its Applications*, 3rd edn, New York 1968, p. 356. Similarly D.R. Cox and H.D. Miller, *The Theory of Stochastic Processes*, London 1965, pp. 212f., 235.

12 Ibid.

13 D.R. Cox and H.D. Miller (1965), op. cit., p. 212.

14 Ibid. p. 38f.

15 William Feller (1968), op. cit., pp. 79ff. The quotation from Feller, 2nd edn, New York 1957, p. 87.

Lecture V Stabilization

Further results on process equilibria and countervailing forces making for mean reversion

Some econometric puzzles resolved

The empirical literature on exchange rates is replete with econometric puzzles which are mainly due, however, to the unreflected application of equilibrium exchange rate theory.[1] Misinterpretations arise in particular when either the initial condition for the interest parity equation is not taken into account or when the one-period nature of the usual uncovered interest parity model is not attended to.

Let us first look at the correlation between interest rates and exchange rates; or, on the other hand, the regression coefficient of interest rates in a regression equation 'explaining' the logarithm of the exchange rate. It is commonly assumed that, according to interest parity, there should be a positive correlation between the interest differential and the exchange rate or a positive regression coefficient of the interest differential in the exchange equation. The logic behind this argument is faulty, however. What happens, precisely according to interest parity if, for example, the home interest rate rises, that is, if the interregional interest differential becomes (more) positive and if, furthermore, the expected exchange rate at the end of the 'period' of the interest change remains the same as at the beginning? At first, home's exchange rate appreciates; after the initial appreciation it depreciates continuously until, at the end of the 'period', it returns to its initial value. But during the whole period it remains in the appreciation range of exchange rate values relative to its initial value, only over time to an ever smaller degree. As appreciation is, in our notation, a fall in the (log) exchange rate, the correlation or the regression coefficient would be negative, not positive, as it frequently is in econometric studies. (That it is not always so is due to the fact that we usually are not in interest parity equilibrium because capital movements on a large scale do take place.)

In fact, we could arrive at the same conclusion also by a simple theoretical argument: basically, the exchange rate is nothing other than the price of two different currencies against each other. If, for example, the stock of money is increased in home, this increases its supply and therefore will, *ceteris paribus*, lower its value relative to other currencies – which implies its depreciation. As a depreciation is a rise in the (log) exchange rate in our notation (and that is the now usual notation) the correlation or the regression coefficient is once more negative.

Now let us differentiate the exchange rate and 'explain' the change in the exchange rate over time by a regression. Surely, if the conditions for uncovered interest parity hold, the regression coefficient will be positive, as uncovered interest parity states that the time change of the exchange rate equals the interregional interest differential with a positive coefficient (of unity; i.e. $\Delta s = \Delta R$)? Not so! For with a positive interest shock of ΔR, there will, as an initial condition, first be a negative initial jump of the (log) exchange rate to the tune of $-\Delta R \cdot T$, if it is fully understood that the changed interest differential will last for T periods. Multiplied by ΔR, this gives $-(\Delta R)^2 T$ as contribution to the denominator of our estimated regression coefficient. Let us call this the statistical period 1 and assume that there are many such small subperiods in our estimation. For the remaining $T-1$ statistical subperiods, the sum of the contributions to the covariance between the (log) exchange rate and the interest differential will be positive, with value $(\Delta R)^2(T-1)$. If the subperiods are sufficiently small, the positive and negative contributions will be approximately equal, i.e. $-(\Delta R)^2 T \sim -(\Delta R)^2\ (T-1)$, and the covariance will be statistically indistinguishable from zero.

Finally, if we take second differences of exchange rates we might assume that the regression coefficient of exchange rates on the interest differential should be zero, as $\Delta_t s = \Delta_t R$ implies $\Delta^2{}_t s = 0$, as long as ΔR remains constant. Not so, once more: only the subperiods of jumps in the exchange rate due to 'innovations' in the interest differential survive as contributing other than zero values to a regression estimation of $\Delta^2{}_t s$. Once more, the regression coefficient should be negative, and not zero.[2]

Another econometric 'puzzle', extensively treated in the empirical literature, is the fact that the forward exchange rate forecasts the future spot exchange rate so badly. In equation (5.1) we restate uncovered interest parity, with the same notation as in equation (3.10), and state covered interest parity in equation (5.2), an equation which is derived by substantially the same logic as uncovered interest parity, but this time actually representing a riskless arbitrage and, therefore, known to hold very tightly with hardly any empirical exception. Let $F^1{}_0$ be the forward exchange rate contracted at time 0 for execution at time 1:

$$(1+R) = (1+R^*) \cdot \frac{S_1^e}{S_0} \tag{5.1}$$

$$(1+R) = (1+R^*) \cdot \frac{F_0^1}{S_0} \tag{5.2}$$

Therefore, taking equations (5.1) and (5.2) together and assuming forecasts which are on average correct, we should have:

$$F_0^1 = E(S_1) \tag{5.3}$$

Actually, however, one usually finds that the forward rate is far from the spot rate at the later date and that, in fact, the two are significantly negatively correlated.

Here, the confusion is due to confounding, on the one hand, the fixed contract period of the forward rate contract (usually, forward rates for three months ahead are studied, though these are by now rather unusual; a seven-day contract being more usual) and, on the other hand, the period during which the initial interest rate differential remains unchanged. Most probably the confusion thus shows traces of bygone times: when interest rates changed rarely, one could safely assume that, on average, the forward rate contract period was shorter than the average period for a given interest differential. But, as shall be argued below, the relevant rates of return now change very frequently so that one can expect a given interest differential to last only for a very short period. Many changes of interest rates will fall inside the time interval of a given forward exchange contract, in particular if we study three-month contracts; and with these frequent interest changes there will be frequent changes in the spot rate within a three-month period. Or, to make this point differently, the assumption that forward rates should roughly correspond to the expected spot rate, as given by the interest parity condition in equation (5.1), at the time of closing a forward contract deal, ignores the high frequency of present exchange rate changes and the relatively large size of the average percentage changes.

Thus, the pivotal point is that the forward contract, by its very nature, holds the initial interest differential fixed (see equation 5.2) while actually it is constantly changing – and changing the spot rate. Technically, index '1' in the spot rate equation (5.1) refers to a different and much shorter period than index '1' in the forward rate equation. For the sake of the argument, let us assume that the home rate of interest R is substantially higher than R^* initially when the forward contract is made. Then, from equation (5.2), the forward rate has to be substantially above the initial spot rate; or formally, if $R \gtreqless R^*$, then $F_0^1 \gtreqless S_0$. However, if $(1+R)/(1+R^*)$ fluctuates symmetrically around unity, or if ΔR, as we called it, has mean zero, then the expected exchange rate S_1 will stay approximately constant, that is, equal in expectation to S_0 and will thus tend to be below the corresponding value of F_0^1; conversely if F_0^1 is smaller than S_0, the expected future value of S will lie above it. The larger F_0^1 relative to S_0, the more it will overestimate the future S_1; and the smaller F_0^1 relative to S_0, the more it will underestimate the future exchange rate. Regressing $(S_1 - F_0^1)$ on F_0^1 will then result in a negative, and substantially negative, regression coefficient. And this is nothing but what one would actually expect from uncovered interest parity.[3]

In fact, there is an important article by McCallum[4] which brings out exactly this point, though in a different way: he explains the failure of the forward rate to forecast correctly the future spot rate with reference to the central bank. He assumes that the exchange rate is mainly 'made' by the central bank, and the central bank is liable to policy reversal: when it discovers that the amount of money has greatly increased, perhaps by chance, it will tend to reduce it in the next period because it thinks such an increase of money excessive and a mistake in terms of longer-run monetary policy, and vice versa. My argument is complementary and founded exclusively on market behaviour. I rely, as it were, on what in comparison one might call 'market reversal', although actually I do not assume a 'reversal' (which would imply negative autocorrelation of interest rate shocks). Much rather, I assume that market movements will be uncorrelated over time. In other words, I just assume a 'back to normal' behaviour of interest shocks, nothing but what was originally called 'regression': after 'drawing' an 'extreme' value of an interest differential, the next drawings are in expectation always again zero, which is the mean for the differential if interest parity should work.

A mere deviation of the expected exchange rate from the forward rate may also have another reason: misapprehensions here being due to a careless interpretation of what 'the' relevant interest rate is. For the forward rate, the relevant interest rate is certainly the short-run rate – by the very nature of the contract. But, as argued at length in Lecture III (pp. 52–3), the most relevant interest rate for the spot rate may be the long-term rate, a rate of return on common stocks or even on real estate and direct investment.

Inflationary shocks not understood by investors

In our basic process model of the development of the exchange rate in the previous lecture, we assumed that market participants fully know the present and all past exchange rates and could fully adjust the nominal rate of interest, given the real one, to this known rate of inflation. Therefore, we could just look at the real exchange rate and the real rate of interest. It was stated there that this was for ease of exposition only. This is to be shown.

Notice that actually not knowing the present rate of inflation is plausible for a very short-period analysis: inflation rates are only measured *ex post*.

Let the rate of inflation, to be called p_t, follow a pure driftless random walk with random 'steps' of ϵ_t per period, ϵ being an i.i.d. variable with mean zero and variance σ^2:

$$p_t = p_{t-1} + \epsilon_t; \qquad E(\epsilon_t) = 0, var(\epsilon_t) = \sigma^2 \tag{5.4}$$

Let us assume that agents form expectations of the rate of inflation, to be called p_t for period t. Let us further assume that expectations are adaptive, which is appropriate for a learning process, in particular if the variable to be estimated is driftless and non-oscillating, as in equation (5.4):

$$\hat{p}_t = \alpha p_{t-1} + (1-\alpha)\hat{p}_{t-1} \tag{5.5}$$

The estimation error of the rate of inflation $p_t - \hat{p}_t$ is:

$$\begin{aligned} p_t - \hat{p}_t &= p_{t-1} + \epsilon_t - \alpha p_{t-1} - (1-\alpha)\hat{p}_{t-1} \\ &= \epsilon_t + (1-\alpha)[p_{t-1} - \hat{p}_{t-1}] \\ &= \epsilon_t + (1-\alpha)\epsilon_{t-1} + (1-\alpha)^2[p_{t-2} - \hat{p}_{t-2}] \\ &= \epsilon_t + (1-\alpha)\epsilon_{t-1} + (1-\alpha)^2\epsilon_{t-2} + (1-\alpha)^3[p_{t-3} - \hat{p}_{t-3}] \\ &\quad \ldots \end{aligned} \tag{5.6}$$

As, by assumption, all the values of ϵ_t are mutually independently distributed, the variance of this estimation error, to be called $\sigma^2{}_M$, equals:

$$\sigma^2{}_M = \sigma^2 + (1-\alpha)^2\sigma^2 + (1-\alpha)^4\sigma^2 + \ldots = \frac{\sigma^2}{1-(1-\alpha)^2} \tag{5.7}$$

The variance is lowest for rationally formed expectations, which would be $p_t = p_{t-1}$, i.e. $\alpha = 1$, and the higher, the slower expectations adapt, i.e. the smaller α.

If the nominal rate of interest R_t is determined according to the Fisher interest equation using an estimate of the real rate of interest, $\hat{r}_t$, and of the rate of inflation, $\hat{p}_t$, we have:

$$R_t = \hat{r}_t + \hat{p}_t \tag{5.8}$$

Let us assume that an estimate of the real rate of interest, $\hat{r}_t$, is correctly derived from known productivities, technical advances and time preferences which, however, change over time. (Without loss of generality we may assume it is estimated without error because any error could be amalgamated with the inflation error.) The estimate of this real rate may be assumed to be independent of the inflation rate. Then the actually achieved real rate, r_t, is given by

$$r_t = R_t - p_t = \hat{r}_t - (p_t - \hat{p}_t) \tag{5.9}$$

The actually achieved real rate of return is its 'real' estimate, $\hat{r}_t$, minus the estimation error of inflation. (It is well known that inflation was frequently underestimated in the past so that the real rate of interest fell with the inflation rate.) Let us now derive the variance of the interregional difference of real rates of return which is relevant for the interest parity condition. Calling this variance $\sigma_\Delta \hat{r}^2$, that of the real kernel of the real interest rate $\hat{r}_t \sigma_{\Delta_r}{}^2$, the variance of the inflation error for foreign (assumed to be independent of that for home) $\sigma_{M^*}{}^2$ and the foreign estimation parameter α^* we finally get:

$$\sigma_\Delta \hat{r}^2 = \sigma_\Delta \hat{r}^2, + \sigma_{M^*}{}^2 = \sigma_\Delta \hat{r}_*{}^2, + \frac{\sigma^2}{1-(1-\alpha)^2} + \frac{\sigma^{*2}}{1-(1-\alpha^*)^2} \tag{5.10}$$

Thus, if inflation is estimated with an error, nothing essential changes in the analysis of our previous lecture. The only difference is that the variance of real rate differentials, $\sigma_\Delta \hat{r}^2$, which is relevant for the size of the jumps of the exchange rate at each interest jump is somewhat more complexly determined.

This derivation makes it clear that 'innovations' of the differential of the real rate of interest between two currency areas are likely to be very frequent: not only changes in productive forces and interest determining changes in productivities matter, but also inflationary shocks. And not only these, but also changes in expectations. Changes in expectations are, however, closely linked to changes in the money supply, which occur very often and with high variance. Money supply changes are important as signals for likely future demand conditions and financial stringency, or the reverse. Furthermore, as I argued in Lecture III, all changes in preferences between types of assets and types of maturities of financial assets may be considered as (real) interest shocks if the yield curves are not equidistant throughout, because changes in the composition of the desired assets change average rates of return achieved. All this implies that we can think of larger and smaller real interest rate shocks actually occurring most of the time.

Does the current account stabilize exchange rates?

The time-honoured classical mechanism by which it was thought that exchange rates will have an inherent tendency to stabilize themselves was assumed to work via their effects on the balance on current account. But for the case of the great world currencies, to which this analysis is alone geared, the mechanisms thought to be at work there are outdated by now. Empirical evidence speaks against them: during the 1990s Japan had alternating periods of protracted and substantial appreciation and depreciation, fluctuations of around 50 per cent in either direction, exhibiting little correlation with the balance on current account which mostly showed a large surplus. And the US-dollar has had a period of marked appreciation in the last few years – at the very time when the current account deficit of the United States reached an unprecedented high.

There are three basic reasons why the current account does not count for much in a world dominated by international capital markets and international capital movements (in other words: for the great world currencies of the most highly developed nations) so that current account effects on exchange rates are easily swamped by other changes in the data. *One*: the theoretical model of the exchange rate process developed in the last lecture shows that it is the real interest changes (or rate of return changes) which provide the basic cause of the temporal instability of the exchange rate. Price level effects are irrelevant. It is the effects of the rates of change of prices, which are rates of return, that count. *Two*: small changes in the relative price levels, which are typical for the non-inflationary world of the leading OECD countries, change exchange rates little in theory, while interest changes expected for a substantial period change exchange rates much. Apart from changes in money demand, which are likely to be small for the small changes discussed, even a permanent 3 per cent rise in the price level of home depreciates its nominal exchange rate in the current year simply by these 3 per cent, and then by 3 per cent in each of the following years, while a 3 per cent increase in the rate of return on assets at home which is expected to last for a mere four years appreciates the home currency already by more than 12½ per cent. In other words: one has to take the likely magnitude of shocks into account. All this would be different, of course, for the world of newly industrializing countries with substantial inflation and not yet fully developed capital markets and relatively smaller capital movements. *Three*: can one really expect the 'tail', namely about 2 per cent current account transactions in total exchange transactions, to wag the dog?

But let us take the arguments presented for the exchange rate stabilizing effects of the current account one by one. The oldest one is, of course, David Hume's *specie-flow mechanism*,[5] which says, in effect, that any deviation from purchasing power parity will rectify itself because of the endogenous changes that it causes in the money supply. If, for example, the price level in home rises, this will throw the balance on current account into deficit. But as an excess of imports over exports has to be paid in terms of money (in contrast to the payment in kind, the payment by exports in the case of balance), money, or gold, will flow out of the country. The supply of money in home will fall and – by the quantity theory – the price level has to fall once more. Thus, a rise in the price level will be self-correcting via the balance on current account and the endogenous change in the money supply which it causes. A real exchange rate deviation from purchasing power rectifies itself.

David Hume explicitly denied any monetary effects on the rate of interest.[6] For the latter he had a theory conceived exclusively in real terms. But by a slight modification we may easily embody his idea into our process model of the exchange rate: a deviation of the real exchange rate from its purchasing power equilibrium causes money flows between currency areas *which lead to countervailing changes in the real interest rates*. If, for example, the price level in home rises, the real exchange rate falls, that is, appreciates, other things being equal; see equation (3.6a) for a constant nominal rate. (As there are countervailing forces and therefore maybe no change in long term conditions, we do not have to assume that the nominal exchange rates need to adjust to this price shock.) The monetary outflow will then raise the real interest rate in home. Initially, this will cause a further appreciation, followed, however, over time by depreciation. If the necessary adjustment process is correctly foreseen, this depreciation will lead back to the original purchasing power parity. Thus, taking the specie-flow mechanism one step further, we realize that a generalized specie-flow mechanism casts doubt on our assumption that the distribution of the shocks of the interest differential is independent of the state variable, the level of the real exchange rate. Not the price level of tradeables as such, but interest differentials have a stabilizing tendency. Note that we can take this analysis even one step further and make it even more general. Even if there is no closed loop from the price level to the balance on current account, and even if imbalances on current account are not due to price level changes but have other causes, there will be a tendency of the real exchange rate to stabilize itself through the workings of interest parity as long as real exchange rate deviations from purchasing power parity cause 'countervailing' movements in the money supply – so that a real appreciation causes a contraction of the real money supply and a real depreciation causes an expansion – and as long as changes in the real money supply have the 'normal' real interest effects, that is, as long as a real monetary contraction causes an increase in real interest rates and vice versa.

Hume's specie-flow mechanism proper (not the modified and generalized version argued in the section above) had some plausibility for his own time and, especially, for a gold currency exchange rate regime. It has been shown, however, that it actually was *not* the stabilizing mechanism of the nineteenth century:[7] compared to the time-consuming and costly process of price adjustments in commodity and labour markets, it was, even then, quicker and cheaper to adjust via interest rates which attracted capital. So, even in the classical gold currency area, current account deficits caused primarily interest rate shocks and capital movements. This was a very convenient way to rectify current account deficits, in particular for the then leading country, Great Britain, which was a creditor nation on a grand scale and partly on a variable interest basis: because a small rise in interest rates in case of a current account deficit tended to rectify this deficit itself immediately due to the fact that it increased the net interest income of Great Britain, which was part of the income account within the current account. Rectifying a current account deficit via interest movements was much more difficult, however, for debtor nations, and in particular if current account deficits raised doubts about their ability to repay their international debts.

Nonetheless, even the modified and generalized specie-flow mechanism is no longer persuasive for the leading industrialized nations. For, with paper currencies, they can easily create an additional money supply internally if there is a foreign drain. So, an imbalance of the real exchange rate relative to PPP need not affect real interest rates at all. Furthermore, the causality may easily run the other way: both high interest rates and the current account deficit may be the effect of a currency area relatively thriving (as compared with other currency areas). High economic growth may cause both high rates of return and a current account deficit because of high levels of demand. The same conditions will cause an appreciation of the real exchange rate. The United States in 1999 and 2000 are a case in question: evidently it was the flourishing capital market, especially the stock market, which caused real appreciation, and that with no considerable effect on inflation; the current account deficit did not cause a depreciation; and there was no monetary contraction, rather the contrary, because there was an inflow of foreign capital in excess of the needs to balance the current account. The current account deficit by itself does not seem to influence interest rates in any decisive way.

The modern (or rather near-modern) argument for the stabilizing effect of the balance on current account on the exchange rate – or vice versa, of the exchange rate on the current account – takes a slightly different tack. This argument is basically Marshallian and Keynesian, amended for capital flows in the Mundell–Fleming model:[8] a rise in the domestic price level by definition appreciates the real exchange rate, other things being equal. The current account is sensitive to the real exchange rate: its derivative relative to the real exchange rate (in the definition used above) is positive so that it turns towards deficit with real appreciation, both of these movements having negative value. A current account deficit causes an excess demand for foreign currency so that the nominal exchange rate depreciates until the real exchange rate has once more returned to its previous equilibrium level and the current account returns to its equilibrium as well. In the meantime, or if the nominal exchange rate does not even tend to adjust, domestic demand is reduced by the current account deficit: the excess of imports over exports. The fall in aggregate domestic demand tends to lower the price level and thus to return it to its original equilibrium. We might add that this fall in domestic demand – by the usual IS–LM argument, with these curves in their 'normal' range – also lowers the rate of interest, which, on the one hand, readjusts domestic demand upwards by increasing investment and, on the other, by its initial effect depreciates the nominal exchange rate. All this is complicated by questions like whether the capital position of the country is positive or negative, how changes in the exchange rate change this capital position and what effects this has on relative demands and on capital movements.[9] There are several adjustment paths, then, all leading back towards or to the original equilibrium. The difference with respect to Hume's specie-flow mechanism is that the amount of money is assumed to be constant. Domestic price level movements are self-adjusting via the current account, and so are exchange rate movements.

But this analysis is outdated, for several reasons. First, if current account transactions make up only 2 per cent or less of the transactions in the foreign exchange market, we cannot expect them to have any considerable effect on the demand or supply of foreign exchange. Current account deficits need not cause a noticeable excess demand for foreign currency; evidently they do not do so in the most recent experience of the USA. But second, and even more importantly: the deficit-enhancing reaction of the current account to real exchange rate appreciation (and vice versa to depreciation) presumes that the Marshall–Lerner condition is fulfilled, that is, that the sum of the absolute values of import and export price elasticities exceeds unity. As, among many others, the Austrian experience from about 1981 to 1998 showed – when the Austrian Schilling was linked to the Deutsche Mark within at first $\frac{2}{5}$ and later $\frac{1}{7}$ of a percentage point – the current account is nearly insensitive to real exchange rate changes, which would imply a sum of import and export price elasticities very close to unity in absolute terms. This would mean that the derivative of the current account with respect to the real exchange rate is approximately zero and the whole argument of the Mundell–Fleming model breaks down.

It is typical for the most highly developed industrial nations to have their sum of (absolute value) import and export price elasticities close to unity: they import above all raw materials which are complementary to home production goods and are difficult to substitute. If, for example, you require copper for various kinds of metal appliances or wiring, you are not likely to use less of it if imported copper rises in price due to exchange rate depreciation. Crude oil, which all highly developed nations import, is known to have had a long-run price elasticity of about 0.3 in absolute terms around the time of the oil 'crises', and at present probably even lower. Other imports are simple consumption goods which are no longer produced at home, e.g. T-shirts. Price elasticities of such 'necessities' are low. So, above all, that argument for substantial price elasticities which says that imported commodities are close substitutes to goods produced at home is no longer valid in most cases.

As to exports, highly industrialized nations tend to export mainly very innovative and highly specialized monopoly products. These are again not very price-sensitive because they are unique. On the other hand, there is well documented pricing-to-market behaviour of oligopolists and monopolists in foreign markets:[10] exporters find it impolitic to vary their price much in foreign markets because of 'menu' costs of price change and because of the danger of 'confusing' consumers. This is true in particular if they think exchange rate changes to be only temporary. They may practise limit-pricing in foreign markets and keep their prices at an unchanging level in order to deter foreign competitors. The 'kinked demand curve' model of oligopoly pricing would argue that it may not be optimal to translate marginal cost changes into price changes; and changes of exchange rates are exactly marginal cost changes for a foreign supplier incurring marginal costs in domestic currency terms in another currency area. To put it briefly: exchange rate changes cause mainly profit variations for exporters, but rarely price changes; and if there are price changes there may not be substantial changes in the quantities sold.

There is a well-known line of argument that exchange rate changes tend to be self-reversing as long as the rates of return do not change. Thus, once more there is no stabilizing tendency to deviations from purchasing power parity as long as interest rates remain unaffected. This has been stated for the case of central bank intervention: it is the analysis of sterilized intervention. When the central bank intervening in the exchange market keeps domestic money supply equal by corresponding intervention in the local financial market, it cannot change the exchange rate.

But the argument is just as true of endogenous market reactions as for interventionist policies. Let us take, for example, the exchange rate intervention of a central bank that wishes to ward off a depreciation of its currency. In order to appreciate its depreciating currency it supplies additional foreign exchange to the market, thus reducing excess demand for it. But this means it reduces the domestic money supply by selling off foreign currency against it. This, however, causes a capital market disequilibrium. Other things being equal, the reduction in the domestic money supply creates a temporary rise in domestic interest rates; this attracts foreign funds, which once more increases the supply of foreign exchange, which had previously been sold, and thus increases domestic money supply to the original level. But the same line of argument holds if private individuals try to speculate about exchange rates. Whether it is the central bank or private agents who try to change the exchange rate, their efforts prove ineffective as long as rates of return and longer-term exchange rate expectations do not change. The capital account reverses all attempts to change a given capital market equilibrium unless medium or long-term rates of return change.

It is doubtful then whether there are any self-adjusting mechanisms at work to rectify deviations of the real exchange rate from purchasing power parity or any other long-term equilibrium to be thought of.[11] But there are some arguments to be advanced that very large deviations which hold for a very long term may have some weak self-regulatory effect. This would imply some limits to the real exchange rate variance in the very long run.

The basic problem faced by those who hope for self-adjusting forces, working on deviations of the exchange rate from its purchasing power equilibrium via the current account, is that short-run flow effects do not count in a capital-account-dominated world with perfect convertibility: if the capital account is fully 'accommodating' in the sense of Meade,[12] capital will flow in and out of a currency area with no noticeable change in interest rates. For, to put it in other terms, it is only changes in interest rates, more precisely changes in rates of return in a more encompassing sense, that count; or, on the other hand, changes in long-run exchange rate expectations, which, as price changes of the financial capital denominated in exchange rates, are once more changes in the rates of return.

I have argued that, in the richest and most highly developed countries, current accounts today show very little price elasticity; that is why the Marshall–Lerner-condition is not fulfilled for them. They are, however, income-elastic to a considerable degree: a large part of the imports, in so far as they are consumption goods, are 'luxuries' or at least not immediate necessities in the short run. In so far as they are industrial raw materials or other industrial inputs, they vary with the more or less thriving state of industry. Exports are reduced when there is a high demand at home for those goods which might otherwise be exported.

However, although the Marshall–Lerner condition may not be fulfilled for relatively small price changes, it may well be fulfilled for very large price changes. As usual, price elasticities depend upon prices. I have argued that oligopolists will practise 'pricing to markets', as has been demonstrated empirically, above all by Knetter.[13] In particular, if they take exchange rate fluctuations merely to be random fluctuations up and down, they may find it either too costly or too disconcerting for their consumers to change their price. But if a change in the exchange rate is very large, they may switch behaviour, especially when large exchange rate changes may well justify the cost of a price change. Or they may altogether stop selling to the currency region in question – with the usual consequences for the current account and for demand and supply of foreign exchange. All these effects will be the stronger, the longer a large exchange rate deviation from former levels lasts. In as far as firms sell innovative products, Lancaster's by now no longer quite so new 'new approach to consumption'[14] would argue that a product has a dominating mix of 'characteristics' only within a given range of prices. Nothing happens to the quantity demanded as long as the price change does not alter the fact that the product in question is dominating in quality. But in case of large price increases, the product finally becomes an inferior choice relative to its possible alternatives: when they are too expensive, even technically superior alternatives are no longer bought. Very large changes in the exchange rate may thus 'sensitize' (potential) customers to change and tend to rectify a current account imbalance. All this would also change long-run exchange rate expectations. Note, however, that the arguments presented would imply that the reaction would be asymmetric: it is too large appreciations which set free countervailing forces.

If we take into account the relatively high income elasticity of the current account balance, we may expect governments to take steps: they may try to reduce domestic demand in order to reduce foreign account deficits. By the usual argument, that would reduce interest rates and thus depreciate the currency as an initial effect. One measure of reducing domestic demand may be to tax business profits or interest incomes

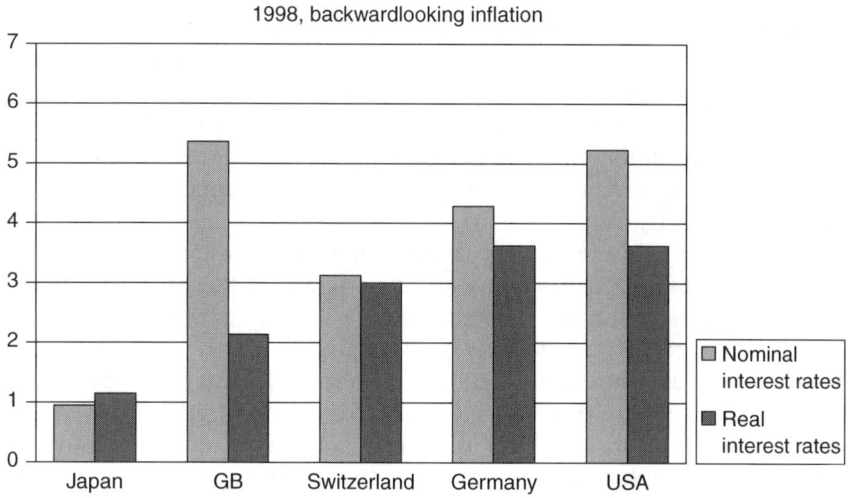

Figure 5.1a Real and nominal interest rates of normally lending and normally borrowing countries. End of 1998, inflation backwardlooking, for four previous quarters.

Lender countries tend to have lower real interest rates than borrowers and therefore in equilibrium currencies which are overvalued, while borrowers tend to have undervalued currencies in order to create the expectation of appreciation.

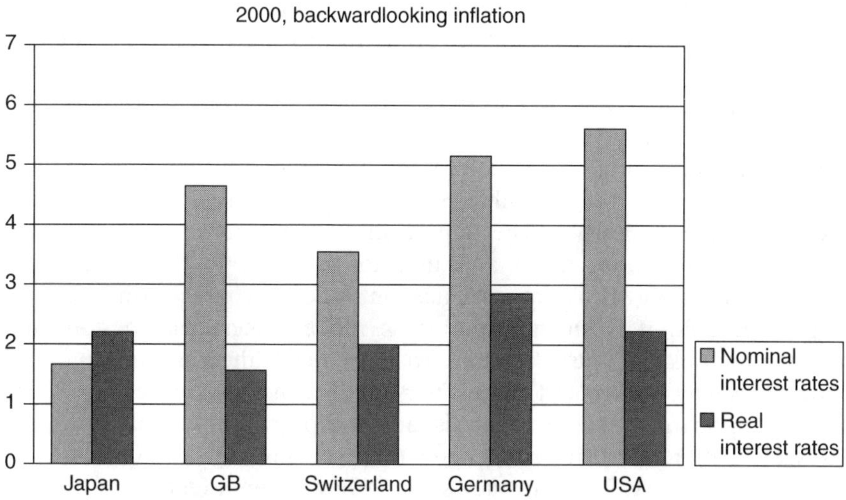

Figure 5.1b Real and nominal interest rates of normally lending and normally borrowing countries. End of 2000, inflation backwardlooking for four previous quarters.

The 'new economy' expectation in the US distorts the picture and the largest borrower, the USA, shows a low real interest rate.

additionally, which would reduce after-tax rates of return. Once more the initial effect on the exchange rate will be depreciating. Note that the argument again works asymmetrically: countervailing government measures are much more likely in case of current account deficits than with surpluses. Note also that, unfortunately, the argument is actually becoming less convincing all the time: the USA are taking no budgetary countermeasures against their mounting cumulative current account deficit of by now 20 years' standing.

But even here there may be a very long-run countervailing effect of long-run cumulative current account deficits or, on the other hand, surpluses. With each current account deficit a country necessarily becomes poorer: it has either to sell assets or to go – more deeply – into debt. The opposite is true for current account surpluses. In international capital markets countries are treated no different from – very large – firms. And a firm that is constantly losing net assets or is going more and more into debt relative to its assets becomes riskier for the outside lender. Thus, by and by and in small steps, a net debtor country will have to pay an increasing risk premium. In the foreign exchange market this may take two forms: either the country has to pay higher interest rates or it has to keep its currency constantly undervalued so that it constantly creates the expectation of an appreciation. Conversely, a cumulative net creditor country will either have to pay a lower rate of interest or have its currency constantly overvalued so as to constantly create the expectation of depreciation. Actually, both of these effects, in an appropriate mixture – effects on interest rates and on the level of the exchange rates – may occur simultaneously in both types of countries so as to provide the appropriate risk premia.

Long-run undervaluation of the currency as adding a kind of risk premium has been extensively discussed as the so-called *Peso-problem*.[15] If a sharp depreciation is expected at an undetermined future moment, with small probability, this possible scenario will depreciate the current exchange rate somewhat. The depreciation is not reversed, even if the 'crisis' expected does not materialize in the current period, basically because the peso problem assumes an indefinite time point for the expected crisis. It is an infinite-horizon model, where one period later everything looks still just the same. Risk premia of the main international currencies may surface as a modest version of such a 'peso-effect'.

This appears to be an analysis not without empirical relevance at present. Until about three years ago a relatively high real interest rate and a relatively undervalued currency seem to have been a feature of the US-dollar; that is to say, until the markets convinced themselves that a 'new economy' in the USA promised higher real rates of return overcompensating the risk of that nation's turning more and more into the largest international debtor. After all, a firm that is going more and more into debt still provides a very promising investment opportunity if it is a particularly innovative firm. That is to say: up to about two years ago, the USA tended to have an undervalued currency and a relatively high real rate of return; and now that expectations have changed, only an even higher real rate of return, at least such a rate of return in expectations. On the other hand, the low interest rates in Japan in recent years and its tendency to have an overvalued yen would provide a perfect example of the cumulative international creditor's fate.

Mounting risk premia thus provide the least abstract hope for a long-run endogenous limitation of the variance of the exchange rates. Actually, however, limitations to excessive long-run deviations of the exchange rate from purchasing power parity have come about mainly because of wars, political upheavals and purely domestically motivated policy changes, especially tax regime changes. This sounds a bit like Malthus' hope placed in 'war, misery, and vice' to limit population, and is nearly as discomforting. Should we really always hope that any currency region with a markedly overvalued currency will be hit by a war destructive of its net international capital position, as the main nineteenth-century creditor nation, Great Britain, was in 1914 to 1918? Should we really hope that particularly thriving nations with overvalued currencies will always become politically very foolish, with devaluing effects on their currency, or countries with a poor exchange rate performance always turn to comparatively very wise – and effective – policies? Should we really always hope that countries with an overvalued currency will always hit upon tax reforms which lower the real rate of return on business, as the USA did in 1985/86? Ever since Adam Smith, economists have placed their hope in some kind of 'invisible hand'. Should we really hope for such a political 'invisible hand' mechanism stabilizing real exchange rates? For actually there does not seem much else to hope for. This point will be more thoroughly discussed in the next lecture.

Interest stabilization

Discussion about exchange rate stabilization focuses too much on the link between the balance on current account with purchasing power parity. But is the short-run flow theory all there is to macroeconomics? Is there today no longer a theory of economic growth, a theory of economic development? – a particularly poignant question to be asked in a series of lectures named after Joseph A. Schumpeter. And as far as interest rates are decisive for exchange rate movements, is there no theory of the real rate of interest behind them?

First, however, a remark about possible monetary causations of real exchange rate movements. The fact that short-run price level changes are not very closely correlated with short-run changes in money, and that short-run price level changes are virtually uncorrelated with exchange rate changes – or, in other words, that real exchange rates tend in the short run to move like nominal exchange rates – need not mean that exchange rates are not strongly affected by monetary changes. In fact, changes in the volume of money yield the best available econometric explanations for short-run exchange rate changes, much superior to changes in price levels. Partly this is so because changes in money have high volatility, as do the exchange rates, while price level changes today have low volatility for the currencies of the most highly developed currency areas. But that this is not due to price level changes being merely longer-term moving averages of money changes (less changes in real output) can be seen from the fact that, when estimated separately, the two coefficients of changes in money in an exchange rate regression equation usually have very different values – contrary to what is to be expected from purchasing power parity.[16] When the USA are one of the currency areas, that is, in cases of estimating any exchange rate with the US-dollar as one of the two currencies, the coefficient for the change in US-money stock is usually by far the larger and often significantly above unity. What may be the explanation for this?

In a world dominated by international finance, in a world of high international capital mobility, the volume of money is likely to become, at least in part, endogenous; and especially so for other countries than the USA. It is no coincidence that Fischer Black used the occasion of his presidential address as president of the American Finance Association to remark: 'I have been unable to construct an equilibrium model in which changes in money cause changes in prices or income, but I have had no trouble constructing an equilibrium model in which changes in prices or income cause changes in money.'[17] If money is endogenous, if its creation is the effect and not the cause of real economic changes, it is quite plausible that it will be used as a signal by foreign exchange markets that real changes are about to take place. It might also be correlated with real rate of return changes without actually causing them. Furthermore, changes in financial conditions, and thus changes in money, might cause disproportionate changes in relative asset prices, which are of great relevance for that 'double asset price', the exchange rate. If changes in money provide merely a signal for real changes in the economy which are larger than its own rate of change, coefficients of the rate of change of money larger than unity in the exchange rate change equation become entirely plausible. And the reason why money changes are used as a signal for short-run forecasting of real economic developments is also clear: monetary changes, at least of base money, are measured weekly and commonly become known immediately so that – on informational grounds – changes in money are the most rapidly available indicator of many other economic changes. No wonder, then, that Clarida and Gali found for both Germany and Japan: 'Our structural estimates imply that monetary shocks to money supply as well as to the demand for real money balances explain a substantial amount of the variance of real exchange rates relative to the dollar.'[18]

All this is true if money is endogenous in the sense of its change being caused by real economic forces. Note, however, that for the short run it would also be true if money is created exogenously and short-run non-neutrality of money holds. For then monetary changes would forecast real economic changes for about a year or two. Increases in money, even if exogenously created, might, for example, forecast higher rates of return of business activity in the near future and thus higher stock market prices and returns, and might thus initially appreciate the currency, even if short-run interest rates fall. It might appreciate the currency if investors (particularly investment and pension funds) are more interested in stock market returns in the foreign currency area than in short-run interest bearing credits. Such an appreciating effect is also likely to occur if, because of capital flows, an increase in the stock of money is just an endogenous consequence of a real economic boom.[19]

The gist of the argument is this: the real rate of return shocks around purchasing power parity (analysed in Lecture IV), shocks which cause potentially ever larger fluctuations, may very well be due to expected rate of return shocks which are caused by changes in the money stock as a signal that the changes in returns are likely to occur. But if money changes are a mere signal of real development then it is unlikely that these signals will follow a random walk independent of the level which the amount of money has reached. In other words: normally, real economic activity fluctuates within relatively narrow bounds. Turning points in business activity become more likely, in particular, when good conditions have prevailed for some time. Thus, both rates of return shocks and monetary shocks as their signal are linked to a more or less cyclical real development and will have a variance-stabilizing bias. On average, the real exchange rate will not deviate ever more from purchasing power parity because the forcing process itself will not show continually increasing variance over time. The exchange rate will show random walk behaviour only in the middle run.

But that was a merely cyclical explanation for variance stabilization. And it was mainly monetary. Should not we assume some stabilizing effects on interest rates to occur in the course of growth and development? Or, to put it differently: are there not long-term real causes to stabilization? Here we have to turn, of course, in the first place to Joseph A. Schumpeter's ideas.

Schumpeter assumed that the rate of interest was due solely to entrepreneurial innovation. 'Dynamic' innovations by 'pioneers' are the cause for non-zero interest rates. When the followers have taken up the new ideas, interest rates once more revert to the stationary level of zero. As was pointed out in the first lecture, this picture has an implausible element. But if we interpret Schumpeterian interest as excess interest above the stationary norm of a non-zero interest level, the picture becomes very attractive. (By the way: it had already been painted by Marx in a much more explicitly argued process, though faulty in parts.[20]) In this sense the real interest rate shocks of the dynamic exchange rate development process in

Lecture IV are due to important innovations (in another, and more fundamental sense than that in financial literature). Because innovations are being taken up by other entrepreneurs and thus become common practice, ever smaller 'excess' interest rates follow a positive interest rate shock. That is to say: a positive 'shock' will be followed by a series of small negative ones. Interest rates will fall back to normal and interest rate changes will not follow a random walk (more generally speaking: a first order Markov process), but will show negative autocorrelation. Destabilizing initial shocks to exchange rates by rates of return due to innovations will restabilize themselves by and by.

But is there such a thing as one single innovation, alone and nothing after, and not much rather a series of successive innovations? May not these have a cumulative effect on the exchange rate? They may, at times. But as far as rates of return are closely linked to the rates of economic growth, this would mean that there would have to be periods of cumulative acceleration in the rate of economic growth or cumulative deceleration, and such periods seem to be rare. Actually, there is an important contribution to economic history which shows that for the case of the English paper industry from the Middle Ages onward and during the eighteenth and the nineteenth centuries, an industry which experienced three large and decisive innovations, these merely meant that its overall industrial growth rate remained just constant over time.[21] (As the Red Queen remarked: 'It takes all the running *you* can do, to keep in the same place'[22] – which could serve as a motto for global competition.) Usually the flow of new innovations is at most just large enough to make up for the terrain lost by old innovations turning into common practice. Rates of return thus remain within a common variance.

Of course, late in his life, Schumpeter argued in this very vein, in his *Business Cycles*.[23] He postulated long-term waves in technological development which he called Kondratief waves. (Today we would probably speak of growth cycles.) Now, it is beside the point for the argument in question whether any such waves exist with any degree of regularity. Usually this has been doubted.[24] What is decisive here is merely the idea that average rates of return, as far as they are technically determined, will remain bounded from below and above, which would mean that the variance of the real rate of exchange, as far as it has technically determined rates of return as forcing variables, will stay bounded around PPP as well.

In Lecture II, I argued furthermore that we can advance an argument *à la* Schumpeter that the average rate of return in an economy is also determined by its rate of bankruptcies: an increasing percentage of bankruptcies serves as a negative, a declining percentage as a positive real interest rate shock. Once more the logic of this explanation would argue for limited variability of net interest rates. For, each firm going bankrupt reduces the number of firms within a constant stock which can still go bankrupt. And even if the stock of firms grows by a process of new entry, firms would become 'extinct' if the rate of 'death' of firms exceeds their rate of 'birth'; particularly so if 'deaths' are accelerating. An alternative argument would be that real rates of return due to the greater or smaller degree of repayment of bank loans can neither fall below zero return for long because then banks would cease to lend, nor could they rise beyond the interest rate at a zero bankruptcy level. So real interest rates which are the mirror image of non-repayment of risky loans will once more remain bounded.

Finally: if high rates of return attract additional capital, the marginal product of capital will fall and thus the real rate of return will decline; and if temporarily low rates of return on capital discourage the investment process, the marginal productivity of capital and thus the rate of return on capital will increase. The static neoclassical world of factor substitution, if it has any relevance at all, would be the sure-fire argument for a negative autocorrelation over time between 'shocks' in interest changes which lead to cross-country interest differences.

My argument was a one-country argument, but the same analysis holds for the two-country case of exchange rates. In fact, it holds even more so: an interest rate shock in one country, if not immediately reflected in the exchange rates to its full extent, will lead to capital movements from or into the other country, and these will tend to reduce any given interest differential.

So, at least in the very long run, there are many forces stabilizing the variance of real interest rate differentials, or, more precisely, differentials in relevant rates of return net of exchange rate changes between countries; and this will tend to stabilize the variance of real exchange rates around purchasing power parity over time. Or, to put our conclusion in other words: the assumption of an i.i.d. process of rate of return differentials is a short- and medium-run approximation untenable for the very long run. And it is only in the very long run that exchange rates do not progressively diverge.

Notes

1 For surveys, see especially Karen K. Lewis, 'Puzzles in International Financial Markets' and Jeffrey A. Frankel and Andrew K. Rose, 'Empirical Research on Nominal Exchange Rates', both in: G.M. Grossman and K. Rogoff (eds), *Handbook of International Economics* III, Amsterdam etc. 1995, ch. 37 and ch. 33, pp. 1913–71 and pp. 1689–1729 respectively.

2 Actually, one can find the second difference of the exchange rate depends empirically upon the time change of interest differentials.

3 For an exhaustive treatment of the vast literature on 'excess foreign exchange returns', as measured by the difference between the forward rate and the actual spot rate at the later date, see Lewis (1995), op. cit., pp. 1916–60.

4 Bennet T. McCallum, 'A Reconsideration of the Uncovered Interest Parity Relationship', *Journal of Monetary Economics*, 33 (1994), 105–32.

5 David Hume, *Political Discourses*, Edinburgh 1752, Discourse V: 'On the Balance of Trade', pp. 79–100.

6 Ibid., Discourse IV: 'Of Interest', pp. 61–78.
7 See Michael D. Bordo and Anna Schwartz (eds), *A Retrospective on the Classical Gold Standard, 1821–1931*, Chicago etc. 1984, in particular John Dutton, 'The Bank of England and the Rules of the Game under the International Gold Standard: New Evidence', pp. 173–95, here pp. 179ff. Furthermore, Barry Eichengreen and Marc Flandreau (eds), *The Gold Standard in Theory and History*, 2nd edn, London etc. 1997.
8 R.A. Mundell, 'Capital Mobility and Stabilization Policy Under Fixed and Flexible Exchange Rates', *Canadian Journal of Economics and Political Science*, 29 (1963), 475–85; and *International Economics*, New York 1968; J.A. Frenkel and A. Razin, 'The Mundell–Fleming Model a Quarter Century Later: A Unified Exposition', *International Monetary Fund Staff Papers*, 34 (1987), 567–620.
9 For a modernized version of the Mundell–Fleming model, embodying sticky prices and using an explicit microeconomic optimizing structure, see Maurice Obstfeld and Kenneth Rogoff, 'Exchange Rate Dynamics Redux', *Journal of Political Economy*, 103 (1995), 624–60.
10 See, e.g. Michael M. Knetter, 'Price Discrimination by US and German Exporters', *American Economic Review*, 79 (1989), 198–210; and 'International Comparisons of Pricing to Market Behavior', *American Economic Review*, 83 (1993), 473–86.
11 See, e.g. various modified PPP values, as the 'NATREX' (Natural Real Exchange Rate) in Stein (1999), or the BEER (Behavioural Equilibrium Exchange Rate) in Peter B. Clark and Ronald MacDonald, 'Exchange Rates and Economic Fundamentals: A Methodological Comparison of BEERs and FEERs', in: MacDonald and Stein (1999), op. cit., pp. 285–322, Lecture II, note 25.
12 Meade (1954) op. cit., pp. 11f. Lecture II, note 6.
13 See note 10.
14 Kelvin J. Lancaster, 'A New Approach to Consumer Theory', *Journal of Political Economy*, 74 (1966), 132–57; and *Consumer Demand – A New Approach*, New York etc. 1971.
15 For the definition of a 'Peso-problem' and a good summary of the literature see Lewis (1995), op. cit., note 1, pp. 1946ff.
16 Already the original MacDonald–Taylor model (1994, op. cit., Lecture II, note 30) estimates on p. 283 coefficients of log money in the log nominal exchange rate equation of 0.209 for m_t (UK, 1976–1990) and −0.498 for m_t* (USA, same period) which are, on the one hand, far away from unity and, on the other, substantially different, with the coefficient for the USA typically much larger. These results can be replicated for many currencies, though frequently with coefficients exceeding unity and not falling below it. Even more variable are results for emerging markets, particularly if their monetary systems are also just emerging. For Malaysia, Thailand, Chile and Mexico see Simon Quijano (2000), op. cit., Lecture II, note 29, who has found quite different coefficients of the money variable towards that of the USA and also quite different variables for different money aggregates.
17 Black (1986), op. cit., p. 539, Lecture I, note 20.
18 Richard Clarida and Jordi Gali, 'Sources of Real Exchange Rate Fluctuations: How Important are Nominal Shocks?', *Carnegie-Rochester Conference Series on Public Policy*, 41 (1994), 1–56, here p. 2.
19 Essentially this was already noted by Harry G. Johnson, 'The Monetary Approach to Balance-of-Payments Theory', in: H.G. Johnson, *Further Essays in Monetary Economics*, London 1972, ch. 8, pp. 229–49.
20 Karl Marx, *Capital – A Critique of Political Economy*, vol. I (B. Fowkes,

trans.) [Penguin Classics] London 1976 (originally in German 1867), Part IV, ch. 12, pp. 433ff.

21 D.C. Coleman, 'Industrial Growth and Industrial Revolutions', in: E.M. Carus-Wilson (ed.), *Essays in Economic History*, vol. III, London 1962, pp. 334–52.

22 Lewis Carroll, *Through the Looking Glass*, London 1871, ch. 2.

23 Joseph A. Schumpeter, *Business Cycles – A Theoretical, Historical, and Statistical Analysis of the Capitalist Process*, New York etc. 1939.

24 Whether Kondratieff-cycles of about 50 years' duration appear anywhere but in the nineteenth-century price level development of some European countries is doubtful. See S.N. Solomou, 'Kondratieff cycle', in: J. Eatwell *et al.* (eds), *The New Palgrave Dictionary of Economics*, London etc. 1987, vol. 3, pp. 60ff., and especially W. Arthur Lewis, *Growth and Fluctuations 1870–1913*, London 1978. For the shorter Kuznets waves of about 20 years' duration, see Simon Kuznets, 'Long Swings in Population Growth and Related Economic Variables', in: S. Kuznets, *Economic Growth and Structure*, London 1965, pp. 328–78, and Moses Abramovitz, *Thinking About Growth*, Cambridge 1989, Part III, 'Long Swings in Economic Growth'.

Lecture VI Mere demand and supply

Stabilization through bounded interest rates and exchange rate theory 'without the contrivance of macroeconomics'

Demand and supply theory without 'fundamentals'

Flood and Rose have called their recent paper, 'Understanding Exchange Rate Volatility without the Contrivance of Macroeconomics'.[1] Have the doubts created by the inability of standard macroeconomic flow models to explain limitations to exchange rate variability, which we discussed in the last lecture, by now mounted so much that we are forced to drop macroeconomic theories altogether?

In this lecture we therefore assume that the exchange rate is a price without anchor because 'fundamentals' are at best known to some traders, and even to those only partially.

In the medium run, exchange rate movements are indeed nearly indistinguishable from random walks. And actually, as has been shown, the real rate of return forcing exchange rate changes is a concept 'so various as to be not one, but all mankind's epitome'. It is therefore legitimate to ask whether we cannot work out an explanation of exchange rate movements that does away altogether with the two usual equilibrium explanations: purchasing power and interest parity. Can we then still say something about the boundedness of variation of exchange rates over time? Curiously enough, we can; and we can do so by using the most incontrovertible and most 'fundamental' of all economic principles: scarcity or the budget constraint.

In a retrospective on his development as an economist, Charles Goodhart relates that he came to exchange rate theory and the 'fundamental' notions behind the usual explanations via the answer he commonly received when asking traders why, in a given situation, the exchange rate had appreciated (or, conversely, depreciated). The traders were apt to resort to the simple answer: 'More buyers than sellers' – an answer totally unsatisfactory to him. In contrast to Goodhart, I think the traders actually had the better answer than the eminent economist. In a pure demand theory model, 'more buyers than sellers' is the key fact.

Now, of course, as economists, we know that in completed purchases or sales there can never be 'more buyers than sellers'. Exchange is reciprocal so that whenever transactions are actually achieved, there are exactly as many buyers as sellers: every buyer finds a seller and every seller a buyer; otherwise, they have not bought or sold.

In a market where participants are extremely uncertain about the relevant information, however, it is most important which party initiates a transaction: is it a potential buyer who wishes to find a seller or a potential seller who wishes to find a buyer? This is important for the process of price change which is triggered by them. A buying order – a bid – may mean that the buyer has information that the price is too low and therefore should rise; and a sales order – an ask order – may mean that it should fall. The kind of initiative, whether a bid or an ask, provides a signal. Such a signal may be perceived today by all but occasional traders: the trading screens they watch provide them with much more information than merely the prices agreed upon.

Glosten and Milgrom[2] have developed such a model of the consequence of bids and asks on price. They are mainly interested in an explanation of the bid–ask price spread. But the model may also be used for our purpose to show the change of price due to the transaction series.

In their model they assume that there are 'specialists' for each financial asset. Specialists post prices for buyers from them and sellers to them. Each specialist is a monopolist; but as the market may be assumed to be contestable, they are (in expectation value) profitless monopolists. For our case we can imagine such a monopolist dealing, for example, in yen against all other currencies. He may actually be dealing only in dollars as the currency on the other side against yen. But we can imagine that, in a well-organized foreign exchange information system, once a yen/dollar or dollar/yen transaction takes place, the prices of all other currencies against the yen are adjusted as well, by instant arbitrage.

With a similar argument we could, with just a little bit of juggling, assume that there is more than one specialist in each currency, but these, always knowing about each other's prices, instantly adjust their prices accordingly when one of them trades, so that our monopolist can be seen as a 'representative agent' firm. Besides, the assumption of a completely profitless monopoly has to be taken with a grain of salt anyhow; for in a stochastic model, as that of the authors named, a profitless firm will go broke with certainty. (Glosten and Milgrom get around this difficulty by assuming their firms have infinite funds.)

At any period of time the monopolist–specialist posts two prices, a higher ask price for customers who wish to buy from him and a lower bid price for those who wish to sell to him; these prices are posted for one unit only of the commodity to be bought or sold. Glosten and Milgrom show that the ask price and the bid price straddle the estimate of the 'correct' value by the specialist (given his information), and may straddle it symmetrically, the bid price lying by just as much below the 'correct' value as the ask price is above it.[3] For, and this is the fundamental idea behind their model, there are two types of participants in the given market: 'noise' traders, who know nothing about the 'correct' value of the asset in question, and 'insiders', who have special information about what the 'correct' price should be. Interestingly enough, the specialist is assumed to be less well informed than the 'insiders' about the 'correct' value of the asset; nor can he distinguish customers as to what they are, whether noise traders or insiders. So because there is the risk that a given buyer is better informed than he, any buyer has to buy from the specialist at the high ask price; and vice versa, any seller at the low bid price. (The prices are so named because they are his, the specialist's, sales or purchase price.)

Thus, whenever a noise trader comes along, the specialist makes a profit; but whenever an insider comes along, he makes a loss. Let us assume that the specialist knows that the probability to be an insider is π and therefore the probability to be a noise trader is $(1-\pi)$. I assume that noise traders, not knowing the correct price, react inelastically to price.[4] Furthermore, I assume that the average percentage excess of the price over the specialists' estimation assumed by insiders is μ. In contrast to Glosten and Milgrom, and as a noticeable simplification of their complex model, I assume that the probabilities π and μ do not change during the process of purchases and sales, i.e. that, due to the constant inflow of new insider information, on average each insider who buys or sells is immediately replaced by a similarly informed insider, at least in the mind of the specialist as to his expectation about purchases and sales. Finally, I assume that the specialist is risk-neutral and interested only in average profits (actually, an inessential simplifying assumption for the general story). For an expected zero rate of profit and thus no reason for the specialist to change his behaviour either *ex ante* or *ex post*, we then get for ϵ, the optimal one-sided percentage spread of the bid or the ask price of the specialist above (or below) his estimation of the 'correct' asset value:

$$\text{Expected profit} = 0 = \epsilon(1-\pi) - (\mu-\epsilon)\pi.$$

$$\text{Therefore: } \epsilon = \pi \cdot \mu \qquad (6.1)$$

There is a pooling equilibrium, as the specialist cannot distinguish between noise traders and insiders and these have no interest to disclose that to him. Or should a noise trader declare: 'I have no idea what the correct price should be'?

If insiders, having information about the price being too high, have the same probability π and the same value of 'sales' information μ as those who believe that the price is too low, the argument is symmetrical for both sides of the spread. We then have: ϵ, one half the percentage spread of ask relative to bid price, or the percentage amount which the ask price lies above and the bid price below the value assumed to be correct by the specialist, is the probability of the specialist to be faced by an insider, π, times the average insider's knowledge of the average percentage short-fall or excess of the 'true' value below or above that assumed by the specialist, μ.

In order to build on the ideas of Glosten and Milgrom I have to point out that foreign exchange markets are particularly rich in noise traders, and noise traders of different kinds. First of all there are exporters and importers who wish to sell their foreign exchange received in the commodity market or buy it to pay their import bills. Basically, they are only interested in current liquidity and it is of little importance to them whether the exchange rate is a bit better or worse. As the accent in this study is on investors' behaviour, exporters and importers will be treated only tangentially; for their demand and supply stream is likely to be unrelated to investors' behaviour. Second, there are investors in the assets of the foreign currency area. Though not essentially interested in foreign exchange as such, but rather in stocks and bonds, in real estate, in buying up foreign firms, the exchange rate is important to them because it is a factor times which their investment prices in foreign vary. They may not form an independent opinion on the likely exchange rate development; but they may take the exchange rate as a signal of profitable (or, conversely, unprofitable) investment opportunities in the currency area in question. Third, there always tends to be a group who sell their foreign asset position (on both sides) for liquidity reasons: inheritance, sickness or retirement make it desirable to turn assets into consumption or consumption-near assets (e.g. savings and time deposits in local currency). The insiders, on the other hand, whose expertise is feared by the representative specialist in the foreign exchange market, are also likely to be of a peculiar kind. Most of the news relevant in the great foreign exchange markets is likely to be news common to all. But the sum of the conditions affecting these markets is exceedingly complex. Therefore, we can say that in the case of the foreign exchange markets news is not information. What counts is how given news is processed, whether the theories used are better or worse, how the news is interpreted. What the specialist therefore fears is an expert evaluator of news who is superior to him. Alternatively, the insider just knows that his (individual) preference for a given currency has changed. And this is the interpretation we shall use in our argument particularly.

What does the specialist in our model do if the last transaction with him has been a purchase? For the next transaction he raises both his ask and his bid price exactly by ϵ per cent, regardless, of course, of whether the last buyer was a noise trader or an insider, which he cannot know. So if the purchaser was a noise trader the price moves (further) away from what the specialist thinks is the fundamental value. But if the purchaser was an insider the price embodies his information, though only part of it: the insiders in this model on average make a profit of $(\mu - \epsilon)$ in percentage terms relative to not their actual, but their average 'true' valuation. So they have an incentive to trade, which would not be the case if the specialist could know they are insiders and bid away their full price information. A mirror-image argument holds for sellers. On average the specialist adjusts his price correctly, over many steps, to the sum of the insider information flowing into the market. He is not disappointed in his behaviour either *ex ante* or *ex post*.[5]

For our purpose, which differs somewhat from what Glosten and Milgrom are interested in, the only relevant element of the model is the step upwards or downwards in the average price posted by the specialist. This step is ϵ; modelled here, as usual, as a percentage, that is, as a difference in price (i.e. of the exchange rate) logarithm. Note that as long as the two probabilities perceived by the specialist, π and μ, remain constant, as I assumed, step ϵ is constant as well. This constant step corresponds to a fixed amount bought or sold. Note furthermore that if the amount bought by a buyer or sold by a seller is not informative about either whether he is a noise trader or an insider or, if an insider, about the size of the misalignment in price he assumes, that is, not informative about his particular excess price estimation relative to μ, it is actually only the number of sales and purchases that counts for price change, not the value of transactions. We can construct a stochastic process of price change with discrete steps, all of the same length ϵ (a discrete state space with unit steps). And it is actually only 'more buyers than sellers', or vice versa, that counts: for every additional buyer a percentage step of length ϵ upwards; for every additional seller, one downwards. Therefore, all we have to analyse is the stream of buyers and sellers over time.

The result would be a simple random walk for the logarithmic price; and if μ, the average excess price, were the same, in absolute terms, for buying and selling insiders and if the probabilities of buyers or sellers to occur were also the same, the random walk would be without drift. We would get exactly the same model as in Lecture IV, page 71, but now for the nominal exchange rate – only it would not be changes in real interest rates driving the model, but more generally the number of buyers and sellers.

Actually, however, such a simple random walk is not yet fully specified; the time dimension of the process is still missing.

The process depends on the rate of time flow of buyers and sellers. Let us therefore assume that the probability of a buyer arriving during a unit interval of time is p and that, symmetrically, of a seller arriving in the same unit time interval is also p; the probability that neither a buyer nor a seller arrives then being $(1-2p)$. As before, the step length of log price change is ϵ, which is determined, as before (see equation 6.1) by the probability π that someone is an insider within the stream of buyers and sellers and his average knowledge of price deficiency μ. Thus, if the process starts at log price zero at time zero and t is time, the variance of the random walk of the exchange rate as a pure reaction to the stream of buyers and sellers, some being insiders, others just noise traders, will be

$$\sigma^2 = 2pt \cdot \pi^2 \cdot \mu^2 \qquad (6.2)$$

The variance increases linearily with time, t, and rate of time flow of buyers and sellers, p, and furthermore with the square of the percentage of insiders within the group of buyers and sellers respectively, π, and also with the square of the insider's excess price estimate, μ.

We can thus expect the variance of exchange rate movements to increase above all with the average volume of trading, p, quite independently from its increase with time, which might not occur because of some restabilizing effect. Furthermore, μ, the supposed deviation of the 'correct' price assumed by insiders, might be a purely subjective notion without true foundation in economic 'fundamentals'. This implies that in times of widely different price estimates by those traders who consider themselves 'insiders' (and are so considered by the specialist in his estimate of their average occurrence), the variance of exchange rate movements will increase: fads make for high variance, a fact to which we shall return.

If we assume, however, that the stream of buyers and sellers per unit of time changes systematically with the level the price has reached, that is, if these streams are state-dependent, we may get a radically different picture. Call the probability per unit of time of a buyer coming along and effecting a purchase, p, and the corresponding probability of a seller arriving and effecting a sale, q. Call $\mu' = p - q$ the mean difference in probability of buyers and sellers per unit of time, our assumption so far having been $p = q$, $\mu' = 0$. μ' would be the drift of the process. Define the stochastic time-dependent price variable as $x(t)$ and its realization at a given point of time as x with $-\infty < x < +\infty$. The price variable is to be normalized in such a way that the 'equilibrium' price $\hat{x}$ is $\hat{x} = 0$, this price being an equilibrium only in the sense that, due to the reaction of buyers and sellers at this price $\hat{x} = 0$, and only at this price, $p = q$, that is, the number of buyers and sellers are equal in probability. (For the sake of convenience we set $\epsilon = 1$ in this submodel.) In general, however, the probability of the number of buyers and sellers per unit of time shall be given by the following mechanism:

$$\mu' = p - q = -\beta x \qquad -p/\beta \leq x \leq q/\beta \tag{6.3}$$

Thus, if the price is below its 'equilibrium' value of zero, purchasers preponderate over sellers; and the more so in a linear functional way the lower the price until finally there are only buyers with the specialist complying with their orders out of his stock. Likewise, if the price is above 'equilibrium', sellers preponderate.

Solving for this process in discrete time and with discrete states we would get the Ehrenfest model.[6] Perhaps better known – and with essentially the same result – are models in continuous time and with a continuous state space.

Let us define in discrete time a random i.i.d. variable Z_t as the difference (or change) in the price variable X between time point t and $t-1$ as

$$Z_t = X_t - X_{t-1} \tag{6.4}$$

If we go to the limit in continuous time the simple random walk with mean drift μ', where in our case $\mu' = 0$, is known to correspond to the Wiener process or Brownian motion with $Z(t)$ being an i.i.d. normally distributed (i.e. white noise) variable:

$$dX(t) = \mu' dt + \sigma Z(t) \sqrt{dt} \tag{6.5}$$

In the present case, however, the instantaneous mean change is $\mu' = -\beta x$. We therefore get the Ornstein-Uhlenbeck process[7] defined by:

$$dX(t) = -\beta x dt + \sigma Z(t) \sqrt{dt} \tag{6.6}$$

While the Wiener process generates a normal distribution with mean $\mu' t$ and variance $\sigma^2 t$, that is, the by now familiar linear divergence in the variance, the Ornstein–Uhlenbeck process generates, with $t \to \infty$, an equilibrium distribution[8] which is normal with zero mean, i.e. at the 'equilibrium' price variable $x = 0$, and with the following variance:[9]

$$Var\{x(t)\} = \frac{\sigma^2 (1 - e^{-2\beta t})}{2\beta} \tag{6.7}$$

$$\text{for } t \to \infty : = \frac{\sigma^2}{2\beta}$$

As our price variable for the exchange rate was in logarithms, the model in this subsection provides a derivation for a stable log normal distribution of the exchange rate, which is frequently found approximately. This model is also an explicit derivation of Friedman's notion of stabilizing speculation,[10] where for some reason or other speculators assume (for example, because of mere social convention) that the 'equilibrium' price is at the value denoted here by $x = 0$ and then behaves according to equation 6.3.

Thus, in modelling theory, it is easy to derive a stable normal distribution of the log exchange rate, and not a time-divergent one: the simple restabilizing behaviour (equation 6.3) makes for such a solution. But why should market participants in reality behave in such a curious way? And if it is the central banks that try to do so, for policy reasons, their reserves are much too small and they would rapidly run out of them.

Contagion

Once we examine models of buyers and sellers in financial markets whose average number is changing over time, models of contagion immediately suggest themselves, contagion providing the reason for such time-varying behaviour or, in other words, models of fads.

Here we can bring in the notion of a limited number of interested investors in each market; or, more or less equivalently, of their budget constraint.

The price development which we shall now analyse is a price at price state x defined as $(1+\epsilon)^x$ relative to the original price. This results because, as before, we take traders' bid–ask spread as given and symmetrical of length ϵ in percentage terms. In logarithms, a price at state x is (approximately) defined as $x \cdot \epsilon$. In other words, we measure price in relative price steps of the specialists, an upward step occurring when one purchase is made and a downward step at any one sale.

The simplest model of contagion is, of course, the well-known 'learning' process or 'catching influenza process' leading to a logistic curve. Actually, as we shall see soon, it is too simple because it is a process of converts only to a given currency, that is, persons who suffer a favourable preference shock, but of no defectors. Furthermore, as it is not a discrete state space model, it confounds the size of the price step per period with the time flow of the number of steps. On the other hand, it allows us to state the time-dependent development process explicitly, which for the stochastic 'birth and death' process analysed below (which is my preferred model) leads to intractable results.

Let us model a contagious preference shift into, for example, yen. The basic assumption in all the models will be that there are only M investors interested in yen at all. So, at most, M investors can shift out of other currencies into yen.

This is a kind of budget constraint. It provides the limiting factor for exchange movements and the reason in the types of models developed here why the variance of the exchange rate remains bounded over time.

At the exchange rate at level x (as defined above), x investors have caught on and have already bought yen. (Note for this case: none have as yet sold. The decision to buy is made once and for all: investors always become 'fully invested' and stay so.) This is a signal to the other investors that it is 'a good thing' to buy yen: the more buyers there are, the likelier is it that a new investor becomes 'infected' with the enthusiasm of such a buyer. Let us assume that each buyer has an attraction on other buyers also to buy at rate λ. The number of those who have already bought thus exerts an impulse, attracting new buyers, to the amount $\lambda \cdot x$. On the other hand, the more investors there are who have already bought yen, the fewer are left who can be attracted into the yen market: only $(M-x)$ are left who can still invest in yen. Thus, (with t expressing time) the rate of change of price x is:

$$dx/dt = \lambda x(M-x) \qquad (6.8)$$

Solving we get (where a is a constant to be determined by initial conditions):

$$x(t) = \frac{M}{1 + a \cdot e^{-\lambda M t}} \tag{6.9}$$

If we assume that, at time 0, $x(0) = \epsilon$, ϵ being the price step per customer, an assumption which also means we are measuring time in the interval between customers, we get:

$$x(t) = \frac{\epsilon \cdot M}{\epsilon + (M - \epsilon)e^{-\lambda M t}} \tag{6.10}$$

so that as $t \to \infty$, x becomes M: the logarithm of the exchange rate will finally have increased by $\epsilon \cdot M$, ϵ being the logarithmic price increase per customer.

Two main conclusions may then be drawn. *One*: whenever there is such a preference shift into a currency, its price rises inexorably to the new level above the previous price of $M \cdot \epsilon$ (in logarithms) and stays there. So the limit price level over time is just this one upper level and no other. But if we step outside the model and assume noise sales, this upper level of $\epsilon \cdot M$ has to be a reflecting barrier because if 'everybody' has already bought, there can only be noise sales and the price has to go down again. As an exchange rate theory our model implies that no other fundamental has to change for price to tend to remain the same or even fall back, apart from the fact that eventually just M buyers have decided to buy. *Two*: the rate of price increase is highest at $x = M/2$, in the middle of the wave of contagion, so to speak, or where just as many investors have already gone into the market in question as are still to be attracted into it (at the point $x = M - x$). So the model also explains variations in volatility, price changing most rapidly around $x = M/2$.

Let us next turn to an explicit stochastic process model of price change due to preference shifts. The appropriate model will be a 'birth and death' model of a population of buyers and now also of sellers. As has been pointed out in the discussion of price change by the exchange rate specialist of ϵ on each purchase and $-\epsilon$ on each sale, this may be assumed to be a discrete state model in (logarithmic) price steps, which are also the inflow or outflow of the number of customers; but, on the other hand, we can assume a continuous time model. Let the probability of a purchase at price level x be called λ_x (where $x = 0$ before the new wave of preference shifts starts); and the probability of sale μ_x. The inter-arrival time or waiting time between customers is typically assumed, and will here be assumed, to be an exponential distribution in both cases, a distribution without memory as to the length of time which has passed since the last arrival. The mean time between arrivals of buyers will be $1/\lambda_x$ and the mean time between arrivals of sellers $1/\mu_x$. Note that if a wave of buyers or sellers waxes or wanes, the representative specialist does not have to change his optimal half price spread, ϵ, because the same percentages of buyers and sellers may be uninformed or informed. The only thing which changes for him is the average number of transactions per period, not the average risk he faces per transaction. (At least, this is the conclusion in the Glosten–Milgrom world where price spread is only determined by information differentials, not for example by a fixed cost for the specialist of staying in business.)

If we once more denote by x the number of steps of length ϵ which the logarithmic exchange rate has made from the initial level zero, and by $P_x(t)$ the probability for the price to be at x at time t, we can state a difference-differential equation for the change of this probability as follows:[11]

$$\frac{dP_x(t)}{dt} = \lambda_{x-1}P_{x-1}(t) + \mu_{x+1}P_{x+1}(t) - (\lambda_x + \mu_x)P_x(t) \tag{6.11}$$

The first term is the appropriate probability of one buyer arriving at price level $x-1$ and thus pushing price up to x. The second term is the probability of one seller arriving at price level $x+1$ and pushing it down to x. So the first two terms make up the total probability of flow into price level state x. The third term, on the other hand, is the probability of outflow out of state x. Together, then, the three terms give the total change.

Unfortunately, for both λ_x and μ_x non-constant and non-zero, solutions for the transient or time-dependent behaviour of this system become extremely messy: they become functions of sums of Bessel-functions of the first kind of order x, difficult to state compactly.[12] So it is common practice to derive only the limiting probabilities $p_x \equiv \lim P_x(t)$. This can be done in our cases because all the systems we study will be ergodic, which is the case if there exists some x_j such that for all $x \geq x_j$ we have $\lambda_x/\mu_x < 1$.

These limiting probabilities p_x of the ergodic (equilibrium) state can be derived as follows:[13]

$$\begin{aligned} 0 &= \lambda_{x-1}p_{x-1} + \mu_{x+1}p_{x+1} - (\lambda_x + \mu_x)\cdot p_x \qquad & x \geq 1 \\ 0 &= \mu_1 p_1 - \lambda_0 p_0 & x = 0 \end{aligned} \tag{6.12}$$

Solving, we have in general:[14]

$$p_x = p_0 \prod_{i=0}^{x-1} \cdot \frac{\lambda_i}{\mu_{i+1}} \qquad x = 0, 1, 2, \ldots \tag{6.13}$$

and derive p_0 from the necessity of all probabilities summing to unity.

Birth and Death Model I. Now the stage is set for our specific model of ‘birth and death’ of customers. Actually, we shall derive three for the sake of comparison.

My preferred model runs as follows: as in the logistic model we assume that new buyers are always attracted, at unit force λ, by the number of investors who have already invested in, say, yen, and in addition they have themselves been convinced to switch. That is to say, the force of attraction is $\lambda(x+1)$. Thus, contagion is socially dependent on previous purchasers. On the other hand, once x persons have bought, only $M-x$ are left to be attracted into the market, M once more being the total number of potential investors. We have:

$$\lambda_x = \lambda(x+1)\cdot(M-x) \qquad 0 \leq x \leq M, \quad x = 0, 1, 2, \ldots \qquad (6.14)$$

The system will be ergodic, as $\lambda_M = 0$, no further inflow being then possible. But now we introduce defectors out of, say, the yen. They may be liquidity traders who just wish to sell anyhow or those who have once more decided that another currency is preferable. Total defection will then be proportional to those who have bought with unit force μ. So we have:

$$\mu_x = \mu \cdot x \qquad 0 \leq x \leq M, \quad x = 0, 1, 2, \ldots \qquad (6.15)$$

Putting the two probabilities of attraction and repulsion together and using equation (6.13), we get:[15]

$$p_x = p_0 \prod_{i=0}^{x-1} \frac{\lambda(i+1)(M-i)}{\mu(i+1)} = p_0 \prod_{i=0}^{x-1} \frac{\lambda(M-i)}{\mu} = p_0 \left(\frac{\lambda}{\mu}\right)^x \frac{M!}{(M-x)!} \qquad 0 \leq x \leq M \qquad (6.16)$$

$$p_0 = \left[\sum_{k=0}^{M} \left(\frac{\lambda}{\mu}\right)^x \frac{M!}{(M-x)!}\right]^{-1} \qquad (6.17)$$

The important point to note is that in contrast to the simple logistic model, all price states from $x=0$ to $x=\mathrm{M}$ occur in this case in long-run equilibrium due to the fact that some investors, who have been attracted into the market, then sell again (we assume they are then 'cured' of their preference for the currency in question until a new wave of attraction, i.e. a new preference shock, arrives). Not a single final price but an equilibrium distribution is the result. In fact, the most probable price lies with $\lambda \geq \mu$ at the maximum level, M, which was the long-run solution in the logistic case or, with $\lambda < \mu$, somewhat below it.

The similarity to the logistic model and the predominance of the probabilities at the very highest levels possible, that is, close to M, would be even more marked if defection were independent of individuals already 'infected', i.e. if $\mu_x = \mu'$.

Birth and Death Model II. A second plausible contagion process of preferences for a certain currency would have this process socially independent, that is, the probability of contagion remains constant at a level independent of previous purchases, but, of course, working only on those individuals who have not yet decided to invest in the currency in question, that is, only on $(M-x)$ individuals. Otherwise the model is as before, being once more ergodic:

$$\lambda_x = \lambda(M-x) \qquad 0 \leq x \leq M \qquad (6.18)$$
$$\mu_x = \mu \cdot x \qquad x = 0, 1, 2, \ldots$$

In this case the solution for the limit probabilities of price states is:[16]

$$p_x = p_0 \prod_{i=0}^{x-1} \frac{\lambda(M-i)}{\mu(i+1)} = p_0 \left(\frac{\lambda}{\mu}\right)^x \binom{M}{x} = \frac{\left(\frac{\lambda}{\mu}\right)^x \binom{M}{x}}{(1+\lambda/\mu)^M} \qquad (6.19)$$

$$p_0 = \frac{1}{(1+\lambda/\mu)^M}; \qquad \binom{M}{x} = \frac{M!}{x!(M-x)!}$$

Once more, in the limit a whole probability distribution of states, not just one limiting state, is the result. Once more the net rate of inflow per period, λ_x/μ_{x+1}, is monotonically decreasing. Thus, in the limit volatility bunching will occur only initially.

This distribution is quite far away from the logistic model. Here probabilites will not be bunched close to the top of the possible range, given by M potential buyers, but around its middle: with $\lambda = \mu$ exactly at the middle, with $\lambda < \mu$ below it and with $\mu < \lambda$ above it.

The two models presented span approximately what might happen and give explicit pictures of preference contagion and their effects on exchange rate distributions. They may provide explanations of the appreciation of the US-dollar relative to the euro in 1999 and 2000. As has been stated already, they are all models of no uniform increase in volatility over time.

Birth and Death Model III. Let us take a very brief look at a model in which the exporters and importers in the currency to which a preference wave is surging are taken into account. Exporters and importers are noise traders in the sense of our model; and noise traders that we might take to provide a constant stream of sales and purchases independent of those of financial investors within a wave of a contagious preference shock. If this preference shock is one into, say, the yen, Japanese exporters will increase the purchases of yen at a rate to be called λ' and importers sales at a rate to be called μ'. Otherwise, everything is to be the same as in our model I. Thus:

$$\lambda_x = \lambda' + \lambda(x+1)(M-x) \qquad 0 \leq x \leq M \qquad (6.20)$$
$$\mu_x = \mu' + \mu \cdot x \qquad x = 0, 1, 2, \ldots$$

If we define $\rho_x \equiv \lambda_x/\mu_{x+1}$ in model I and $\rho'_x \equiv \lambda_x/\mu_{x+1}$ in model III, we have

$$\rho'_x = \frac{\lambda' + \lambda(x+1)(M-x)}{\mu' + \mu(x+1)} = \frac{\dfrac{\lambda'}{x+1} + \lambda(M-x)}{\dfrac{\mu'}{x+1} + \mu} \tag{6.21}$$

$$\rho'_x \gtreqless \rho_x \text{ iff } \frac{\dfrac{\lambda'}{x+1} + \lambda(M-x)}{\dfrac{\mu'}{x+1} + \mu} \gtreqless \frac{\lambda(M-x)}{\mu} \tag{6.22}$$

As is seen immediately, for large M and $x \to M$, the net rate of inflow, ρ, into a given currency will hardly differ from model I, because λ/M and μ/M are most likely to be very small. On the other hand, for x close to zero the difference is likely to be substantial for M large, no change at $x = 0$, implying $\lambda'/\mu' = \lambda \cdot M/\mu$. So the net rate of inflow and the equilibrium probabilities are likely to be smaller at low values of x. In other words, such an additional constant flow of noise traders makes the process of model III conform more closely to the logistic, because the additional sales of the currency due to imports, μ', make low levels of exchange rate increase relative to the initial level less likely.

Misunderstanding different opinions and risk

Once we have traders of different information levels, even sudden chaotic jumps up and down of the exchange rate become quite likely. The two most interesting and mature models of such chaotic jumps were presented by Genotte and Leland[17] and by David Romer.[18] Both are actually explanations of the Wall Street stock market crash in October 1987, a drop of about 20 per cent in index terms. But they are equally applicable to sudden exchange rate swings, either directly or because of changes in prices of the underlying financial assets. A case to be explained thereby, for example, would be the 15 per cent appreciation of the yen within a few hours on October 7, 1998.

I find the Genotte and Leland explanation particularly persuasive. They introduce a new and possibly quantitatively very important type of trader who might also be termed a noise trader: a trader who merely adjusts portfolios in such a way that the new relative quantity of assets remains optimal after a price change, that is follows so-called portfolio insurance strategies. If the price of an asset has fallen, the optimal strategy is to reduce the quantity of this asset held in the portfolio. But the other traders misinterpret such mere ‘automatic’ quantity adjustment as a sign that the traders in question have received bad ‘news’: after all, these are important traders who ought to be in the know! Thus, a small reduction in prices can lead to a stampede and a chaotic price rise or drop. One type of trader takes as a signal of likely further price change what is only a mechanical adjustment to past price change.

David Romer, on the other hand, assumes several levels of information between traders. The better a trader is informed the higher he weights his own information relative to that which the market tells him the other traders have. Shifts in price can now tell traders whether they are better or worse informed than they previously thought. This may lead to sudden readjustments of the weights given to one's own information and that attributed to others and thus to sudden price shifts: without any 'news' the market may readjust. To me, this seems a less convincing explanation because in an ongoing trading process participants should have found out already how well they are informed.

So do these models provide persuasive explanations of 'bubbles' in asset prices in general and in exchange rates in particular? The answer is: no. A 'bubble' presupposes a 'fundamental' price from which actual prices are deviating for reasons of self-fulfilling expectations. But (as has been emphasized again and again in these lectures) in case of non-renewable or costlessly renewable international assets, and of foreign exchanges in particular, there does not exist any long-term 'fundamental' price independent from the momentary market estimations. There is no measuring rod against which a 'bubble' may be defined. As such, it is pure 'normality'. What may be the case is that prevalent expectations may be seriously disappointed, but that is all.

Another frequently stated criticism is that exchange rates imply much too large and too rapidly varying risk premia. Once more, risk premia are calculated with respect to notions of equilibria which frequently are unrealistic. But even if we can accept these measuring rods, it should be remembered that risk premia in foreign exchange transactions must not be calculated relative to average consumption and average net wealth. Exchange rate holding strategies are very often entirely or almost entirely credit-financed. And, as was pointed out in Lecture II, in case of net worth positions close to zero, risk premia must be assumed to be very high. Since foreign exchange markets are not efficient, net worth positions matter. Long-Term Capital Management found that out to its distress.

The low average net worth and thus the high risk premia are also the reason why, for very risky currencies, in particular the yen, average appreciation is substantially less than the interest differential over long periods. And that means that debtors with a risk aversion much below average and going into debt for unusually long periods (i.e. issuing bonds for ten and more years) on average may gain substantially in these markets. In other words, it is sensible in particular for governments to issue yen and also Swiss franc bonds.

Varian[19] has pointed out another interesting phenomenon. Assuming for once efficient financial markets, he has demonstrated that a greater divergence of opinion about the probabilities of future states of the world (greater divergence in the sense of a higher mean preserving spread) leads to a lowering of the price of the asset in question, if relative risk aversion is larger than one, which is, empirically speaking, highly likely. So greater uncertainty about its future will lead to depreciation in the exchange rate. This – in addition to the improvement of opinions about the prospect of the dollar, which may have been a fall in diversity – may be a main reason for the depreciation of the newly introduced euro in 1999: during that year uncertainties about the likely financial policies of Euro-Europe increased and opinions about the likely future of the euro diverged.

In this lecture, I have shown that in the case of exchange rates monetary and real forces are hopelessly entangled. In fact, it makes no sense even to try to distinguish between them. For monetary effects, even on real exchange rates, may be permanent, or at least as 'permanent' as anything is in an uncertain world. And so-called real effects may prove to be temporary. In addition, pure demand and supply mechanisms cannot distinguish between 'real' and 'nominal'. Thus, nominal exchange rates provide the most potent source of non-neutrality in integrated financial markets and a basically anchorless nominal exchange rate system. They make money non-neutral, even in the long run – a phenomenon which will concern us in the next (and final) lecture.

Notes

1 Robert P. Flood and Andrew K. Rose, 'Understanding Exchange Rate Volatility Without the Contrivance of Macroeconomics', *Economic Journal*, 109 (1999), F660–F672.

2 Lawrence R. Glosten and Paul R. Milgrom, 'Bid, Ask and Transaction Prices in a Specialist Market with Heterogeneously Informed Traders', *Journal of Financial Economics*, 14 (1985), 71–100.

3 Ibid., Proposition 1, p. 80f.

4 Glosten and Milgrom (ibid.) assume price elasticity of noise traders. But if these are faced with a liquidity need, which is the usual rationalization of 'noise' trading, this would seem to be a contradictory assumption. Anyway, a non-zero price elasticity of trading just complicates the model unnecessarily.

5 Actually, this statement is not quite correct: insiders who differ too little in their price estimate from the specialist, i.e. whose price estimate differs by less than or just by ϵ from his, do not trade.

6 See Cox and Miller (1965), op. cit., pp. 129ff. Lecture IV, note 11.

7 See ibid., pp. 207f., 226ff.

8 I have examined a similar model for the required quantity of foreign exchange reserves in: Erich W. Streissler, 'A Stochastic Model of International Reserve Requirements During Growth of World Trade', *Zeitschrift für Nationalökonomie*, 29 (1969), 347–70, here pp. 367f. Ball and Roma (1993), op. cit., Lecture II, note 34, also use an Ornstein-Uhlenbeck modelling structure for mean reversion.

9 Cox and Miller (op. cit.), formula (100) on p. 226.

10 See Lecture II, p. 20.

11 Leonard Kleinrock, *Queueing Systems*, Vol. I: Theory, New York etc. 1975, pp. 57 and 59.
12 Ibid. p. 77f.
13 Ibid. p. 90.
14 Ibid. p. 92.
15 Ibid. p. 106f.
16 Ibid. p. 107f.
17 Gerard Genotte and Hayne Leland, 'Market Liquidity, Hedging, and Crashes', *American Economic Review*, 80 (1990), 999–1021.
18 David Romer, 'Rational Asset-Price Movements Without News', *American Economic Review*, 83 (1993), 1112–30.
19 Hal R. Varian, 'Divergence of Opinion in Complete Markets: A Note', *Journal of Finance*, 40 (1985), 309–17.

Lecture VII Non-neutrality

On the neutrality of money – or: the story of Anacharsis the Scythian

The problem

Economists have developed important assumptions which isolate large fields of analysis from one another. This is essential for the organization of research in a discipline ever more split up into highly specialized subdisciplines. The scholar in long-run 'real' macroeconomics need not follow in detail what people in monetary economics do because, due to the long-run neutrality of money, purely financial developments need not concern him. Another such isolating assumption has been, ever since John Stuart Mill, the dichotomy between distribution and efficiency (or production) though we feel a little more uneasy with this cleavage today. One might even suggest that, above all, perfect competition or complete information are such assumptions isolating subdisciplines.

Such isolating assumptions are quite useful and may even be necessary tools of the trade. They build a fence beyond which one need not look. The trouble with them is, however, that on one side of the fence developments may take place which, unnoticed by scholars on the other side of the fence, cast serious doubts on the crucial isolating assumption. And that is just what is happening now – or once more – with the central premise of the long-run neutrality of money. Once more, monetary developments are becoming very important for the 'real' economy.

This is best seen perhaps in the field of economic policy. If you suggest to a central banker, well trained in economics, to Otmar Issing, for example, or Mervyn King, that he should do something to lower long-term interest rates, substantially and for an extended period, in order to stimulate investment, he will probably lecture you that only the real rate of interest is relevant for investment and that, due to the long-run neutrality of money, monetary policy cannot affect this real rate of interest in the long run. Some years ago at a conference of the International Economic Association, when a significant 'unorthodox' French economist suggested that the high rate of unemployment in France was due to the Bundesbank pushing up the real rate of interest – this was in 1997, when it was still plausible for the real rate of interest to be unusually high – I heard Robert

E. Lucas, Jr. (to the delight of Otmar Issing, also present), absolutely congeal the atmosphere with the remark: 'Is there anyone in this room not knowing that money is neutral, after so many studies showing it to be so?' Suggest then to a central banker, on the other hand, that he is a mere short-run technician and not a politician of any significance, for actually he can effect nothing of real importance: he will immediately turn round to tell you, no, a steady, good, orthodox monetary policy is quite influential. It will reduce uncertainty, may even lower the risk premium as a constituent part of (real) interest rates and will thus affect economic growth most favourably. So it is quite common today to have one's monetary cake and eat it too; or, in other words, it is common either heavily to depend on the neutrality of money or to ignore it, as the occasion demands.

I do not wish to suggest that these two lines of argument, though contradictory, are not 'correct' simplifications, correct in the sense that they point to the most important and most easily manipulated causes. Actually, I believe, a fuller argument would state that some central banks can affect the real interest rate even during a considerable medium-term period; their effectiveness depends on their credibility and the expectations and beliefs they generate. But it is much too difficult, because too variable over time and circumstances, to understand by what measures all this can be achieved and in what direction the long-term real interest rate will go; not at all necessarily in the direction suggested by a Keynesian-type analysis. So it is best to say the central bank cannot affect the real rate of interest. Probably, the 'Fed' under Greenspan has prolonged a boom in the United States from at least 1998 onwards until 2000 (or longer?) and has affected real interest rates through its effect on the stock market. But could the ECB have done the same?

Here, we may run up against about the worst kind of non-neutrality of money for a central bank: the effects you create depend upon *who you are*, whether you are the 'Fed' or some other central bank. And the most important non-neutrality today is the very long-term deviation of exchange rates from purchasing power parity.[1] Exchange rates are mainly monetarily determined, but behave in a decidedly non-neutral way for very long periods. Furthermore, their high degree of volatility has real effects, in other words: not only mean values but also variances have real effects.[2] These facts furnish the empirical reasons behind this lecture: exchange rate behaviour is not yet integrated into the theory of monetary neutrality.

There is one more incident among important economists that I should like to relate in order to focus attention: in a meeting of the International Economic Association in Buenos Aires on Tuesday, August 24, 1999, John P. Taylor presented a masterful summary of what the effect of various kinds of policy rules ('Taylor rules') followed by central banks would be on a number of real macroeconomic variables. In the discussion Kenneth J. Arrow rose and asked why Taylor had not analysed the effect central bank policy might have on long-run employment, capacity utilization, and growth. Taylor became somewhat apologetic and said he had only gone through the cyclical effects monetary policy would generate, while as to growth, you know, in the long run money is neutral.[3] Thus, apart from neutrality, he used a second well-worn and also highly problematic isolating assumption: the independence of the growth trend from the cycle. The Nobel laureate was not satisfied. But what is perhaps more interesting: how could he pose his question in the first place? Is not the Arrow–Debreu model – or a variant of it – *the* reference point for the modern interpretation of the neutrality of money? Could it be that the author, Kenneth Arrow himself, thinks much less of the applicability of his general equilibrium model to solve economic conundrums that lie at the bottom of many other types of theories as well as at the heart of many important problems of economic policy? May we even invoke a possible general theorem that real-life general equilibrium theorists tend to be much more sceptical about the 'comforting truths' of general equilibrium theory than outsiders to that select group?

Neutrality as expounded by Hume

But let us first turn to the origins of the idea of the neutrality of money, if only to see that the common argument among monetary economists today does not differ in the least from that already laid down in the middle of the eighteenth century. The argument is British and nearly as old as modern economics.

For the idea that the rate of interest is primarily a monetary phenomenon and not directly determined by real forces we would now probably quote Keynes: 'The rate of interest is not the "price" which brings into equilibrium the demand for resources to invest with the readiness to abstain from present consumption. It is the "price" which equilibrates the desire to hold wealth in the form of cash with the available quantity of cash.'[4] In eighteenth-century Britain, Keynes' 'pseudonym' was John Locke. Locke (1692)[5] states as a bald fact, repeatedly but without any clearly discernible reasoning, that a larger amount of money would lower the rate of interest, thus stimulating the economy in a by then well understood way. Previously, Josiah Child had already argued forcefully – his 'pseudonym' in present-day continental Europe is Jean-Paul Fitoussi – that lowering the rate of interest by government fiat, or in some other unexplained way, would, indeed, vastly benefit the economy. So, in that sense Locke's argument was a decided advance in economic thinking; for he presented an economic mechanism for lowering the interest rate. Nevertheless, for such a profound and clear mind as that of Locke, his analysis is very badly presented, merely a repeated assertion – the important contribution of his essay being that it first introduced the notion of the velocity of the circulation of money. In these parts of his essay Locke also argued that the relative volume of monetary circulation – relative, that is, to the quantity of goods – would change all prices. In spite of its wobbly (and, at base, even contradictory) presentation, his argument soon became a *locus classicus*.

In contrast Cantillon (around 1730),[6] author of a marvellous economic treatise, 'from whom Quesnay, Sir James Steuart & A. Smith have largely drawn',[7] presented a 'real' explanation of the rate of interest: it is determined by the desire to invest – Cantillon says: by the number of entrepreneurs – relative to the volume of saving. Explicitly, interest has no 'necessary' relationship with the (relative) amount of money in a country. In contrast to Locke he tried to show the exact mechanism by which money raises prices: but with him this process is non-neutral,[8] even in the long run: the constant inflow of money (i.e. silver and gold) from the Americas ruined Spain, which became non-competitive, as prices rose most at the point of monetary injection. By and by, to put the argument in modern terms, the monetary inflow changed the preferences of the Spaniards and made them unlearn valuable techniques of production (mainly they became soldiers subservient to the sovereign, who had received all that money in the first place).

Cantillon, it must be said, is highly readable even today: in the main his is an asset approach to money, expectations explicitly playing an important role with their altogether variable effects.[9] We could summarize Cantillon as follows: there are mixed monetary and real effects on the rate of interest, but mainly the latter.

This is where matters stood when the young David Hume took up these questions in his *Political Discourses* (1752). To say that Hume is the eighteenth-century 'pseudonym' for Milton Friedman would be unjust to Hume. Much rather, Friedman is the 'pseudonym' under which Hume's arguments run in the twentieth century: for Hume already presented all the now standard arguments on the neutrality of money.[10] And in rereading his essays one can study admirably how badly they fit together. Two or three of his *Discourses* pertain to monetary matters: Discourse III, 'Of Money', Discourse IV, 'Of Interest', and in a way Discourse V, 'Of the Balance of Trade', with the famous price–specie flow equilibrating mechanism of the balance of trade.

The long-run neutrality of money, though not the short-run, and the effect of money on prices, is argued by Hume in Discourse III; but it is then restated most clearly in Discourse IV, 'Of Interest', to which we shall therefore turn first. After all, for practical purposes of policy, the absence of an effect of money on the real interest rate is still the central issue of monetary neutrality.

Hume starts the essay thus:[11]

> Nothing is esteem'd a more certain sign of the flourishing condition of any nation than the lowness of interest: And with reason; tho' I

> believe the cause is somewhat different from what is commonly apprehended. The lowness of interest is generally ascrib'd to the plenty of money. But money, however plentiful, has no other effect, *if fixt*, than to raise the price of labour.... Were all the gold in England annihilated at once, and one and twenty shillings substituted in the place of every guinea, wou'd money be more plentiful or interest lower? No surely: We shou'd only use silver instead of gold ... No other difference wou'd ever be observ'd. No alteration on commerce, manufactures, navigation, or interest; unless we imagine, that the colour of the metal is of any consequence.
>
> Now what is so visible in these greater variations of scarcity or abundance of the precious metals, must hold in all inferior changes. If the multiplying gold and silver fifteen times makes no difference, much less can the doubling or tripling them. All augmentation has no other effect than to heighten the price of labour and commodities; and even this variation is little more than that of name. In the progress towards these changes, the augmentation may have some influence, by exciting industry; but after the prices are settled, suitable to the new abundance of gold and silver, it has no manner of influence.
>
> Money having merely a fictitious value, arising from the agreement and convention of men, the greater or less plenty of it is of no consequence, if we consider a nation within itself; and when once fixt, tho' in never so great abundance, it has no other effect, than to oblige every one to tell out a greater number of those shining bits of metal, for cloaths, furniture, or equipage, without encreasing any one convenience of life...
>
> High interest arises from *three* circumstances: A great demand for borrowing; little riches to supply that demand; and great profits arising from commerce...

And after telling us: 'low interest ... proceeds from the three opposite circumstances', Hume goes on persuasively to explain to us his purely real theory of interest over 15 more pages.

Note five points in this statement of monetary neutrality by Hume, all of them still very much with us today. *First*, in the long run no effects on relative prices will be due to the amount of money, 'if fixt' – Hume's text has italics here. But actually, at present it is an extremely complicated informational problem to understand whether the amount of money remains constant. *Second*, the temporary effects on relative prices are without consequences for the long run. But why would that be so? This is so because, *third*, eventually 'the prices are settled', evidently in a unique, and unchanged, 'real' equilibrium. This may be the trickiest point of all, as we shall scc. It is evident that Hume has a general equilibrium theory of prices at the back of his mind, the price theory of Diocletian, as I called it in Lecture I. *Point four*: in this, and in other instances (especially in his doubts on the real value of paper credit and of banks, quite in contrast to his younger friend, Adam Smith[12]) Hume seems to imply that even changes in monetary institutions are neutral with respect to relative prices in the long run: with him a switch from gold to silver has no real effect; and explicitly he entertains 'a great doubt concerning the benefits of banks and paper credit'.[13] But why then have we introduced the euro now in continental Europe? As every child knows, transaction costs may change with another denomination of money or with large enough changes in the availability of money, brought about by changes in the quantity of money in circulation. So Hume is even more neutralist than monetary neutralians would be today. Finally, and *fifth*, Hume argues for neutrality because 'Money (has) merely a fictitious value', which is tantamount to Walras' 'numéraire' argument. But he adds a tell-tale remark which he had better suppressed for the sake of his argument: This 'fictitious value [arises] from the agreement and convention of men'. Cannot such social 'conventions' change? What happens if each and everybody changes expectations?

Thus, from its very start the theory of monetary neutrality has loose ends which are not perceived, however, as long as one has a certain picture of economics in mind; or, to put it differently, as long as social life is such that, in particular, markets for international financial assets do not play too vital a role and are not too closely linked to changes in the amount of money – or the many moneys world-wide? All this becomes even clearer if we turn to Hume's Discourse III, 'Of Money', where the case for monetary neutrality is first argued.

This essay starts out with the assertion: 'Money is not, properly speaking, one of the subjects of commerce; but only the instrument, which men have agreed upon to facilitate the exchange of one commodity for another. 'Tis none of the wheels of trade: 'Tis the oil, which renders the motion of the wheels more smooth and easy.' Today we would say: according to Hume, money as such has no utility. And curiously, while being 'the oil [for] the wheels', it does not seem to change transaction costs, a notion alien to Hume, though not to the mercantilists before him.[14]

Hume briefly states his main point then, which one might call the central idea of classical economics, to be codified about a quarter of a century later by Adam Smith: 'The greater number of people and their greater industry are serviceable in all cases; at home and abroad, in private and public life. But the greater plenty of money is very limited in its use, and may even sometimes be a loss to a nation in its commerce with foreigners.' (Of course, the latter point is the long-run negative non-neutrality of the inflow of money from the Americas for the Spaniards, a social topos of the times and discussed at length by Cantillon, who was certainly known to Hume.)

Hume then goes on to present the unit of account aspect of money, suggesting implicitly that this is substantively the only function of money.[15]

> 'Twas a shrewd observation of *Anacharsis* the *Scythian*, who had never seen money in his own country, that gold and silver seem'd to him of no use to the *Greeks*, but to assist them in numeration and arithmetic. 'Tis indeed evident, that money is nothing but the representation of labour and commodities, and serves only as a method of rating or estimating them. Where coin is in greater plenty; as a greater quantity of it is then requir'd to represent the same quantity of goods; it can have no effect, either good or bad, taking a nation within itself: no more than it wou'd make an alteration on a merchant's books if instead of the *Arabian* method of notation, which requires few characters, he shou'd make use of the *Roman*, which requires a great many.

The notion that money is merely a 'numéraire' is, of course, the ideal basis for the theory of the neutrality of money. So, following Hume, let us call this the theory of Anacharsis the Scythian. But the question is: is the theory of Anacharsis the Scythian still good enough today? Hume, in fact, immediately has the greatest difficulty with his own theory, as he shows us half a page later:

> We find, that in every kingdom, into which money begins to flow in greater abundance than formerly, every thing takes a new face; labour and industry gain life; the merchant becomes more enterprizing; the manufacturer more diligent and skillful; and even the farmer follows his plough with greater alacrity and attention. This is not easily to be accounted for, if we consider only the influence, which greater abundance of coins has in the kingdom itself, by heightening the price of commodities, and obliging every one to pay a greater number of these little yellow or white pieces for every thing he purchases...

And, indeed, if you hold a mere unit of account theory of money, 'this is not easily to be accounted for'. Hume holds a theory of the neutrality of money in the long run relative to the level of the quantity of money – namely, the '*if fixt*' argument. But he assumes that the rate of change of money is not neutral. Although conversant with the copious literature on the – (usually) lack of – superneutrality of money about 30 years ago, I find it difficult not to see a contradiction here.[16]

As is well known Milton Friedman, Hume's 'pseudonym' in the twentieth century, has argued that the short-run non-neutrality of money is due to mistaken assumptions about the ruling prices – or the prices soon to rule – by economic agents.[17] Here, the question arises: if they have wrong perceptions in the short run, why should these not persist in the long run if circumstances are sufficiently complex, as they are on international financial markets at present? To my mind, Hume has a better argument, and one much used today in the literature on menu costs. He says:

> To account, then, for this phenomenon, we must consider, that tho' the high price of commodities be a necessary consequence of the encrease of gold and silver, yet it follows not immediately upon that encrease; but some time is requir'd before the money circulate thro' the whole state, and make its effects be felt on all ranks of people. At first, no alteration is perceiv'd; by degrees, it raises the price first of one commodity, then of another, till the whole at last rises to a just proportion, with the new quantity of specie, which is in the kingdom. In my opinion, 'tis only in the interval or intermediate situation, betwixt the acquisition of money and rise of prices, that the encreasing quantity of gold and silver is favourable to industry. When any quantity of money is imported into a nation, it is not at first disperst into many hands; but is confin'd to the coffers of a few persons, who immediately seek to employ it to the best advantage...

None of Friedman's helicopters here. But why should prices eventually all rise proportionately? One of Hume's problems (in his also flawed 'balance of trade' argument) is that he does not distinguish between commodities in international competition, on the one hand, and those monopolistically supplied or pure domestic goods, on the other. The first cannot rise in price, unless the exchange rate changes exactly with the additional relative amount of money in the country, that is, if relative purchasing power parity holds, which it does not over very long periods. And what if, meanwhile, prices of financial assets follow a random walk? All of the difficulties of Hume's argument are still with us, and they are ever more alive and well.

Note, finally, that if you base neutrality on the mere unit-of-account notion of money, as Hume does, you have no relationship whatsoever between the quantity of money and prices left, be they nominal or real. Money is then a mere idea, whose physical quantity is completely immaterial.

Hume's analysis was never forgotten by economists and frequently used by classical and neoclassical authors – although it was not taken too seriously. Of course, the key questions were: which commodity is money? Or, even more pointedly, which of many commodities can be designated more or less as money? And what do the economic agents expect their effects to be? – a question not at all otiose if certain assets have prices without any necessarily firm 'anchor', that is, without a stable equilibrium value. In other words, with 'money having merely a fictitious value, arising from the agreement and convention of men', as Hume put it, neutrality can be at best an approximate attribute of money, and that only under certain institutional and historic circumstances.

In spite (or even because) of the fact that the term 'neutrality of money' probably originated with the Austrians,[18] all the members of that school held at best a vacillating position. In fact, in his monumental and still untranslated article, 'Geld' (i.e. 'Money')[19] the founder of the school, Menger, showed an outright non-neutralian stance, denying any stability of the velocity of circulation, if not the usefulness of that concept altogether: most money is held 'in the form of manifold reserves in order to safeguard against uncertain, in many cases actually never occurring payments'.[20] Friedrich von Wieser defined money as being characterized by 'habitual mass acceptance' (habitual mass use);[21] in other words: quite conventionally. And Haberler at the very end of the school thought that 'the response mechanism [to money] is more important than "quantitative changes"'.[22]

So let us next take a huge jump in time from the eighteenth and the nineteenth centuries and turn to the near-modern arguments on the neutrality of money around the time of Don Patinkin's seminal publication (1956).[23] These are based on the post-war notions of General Equilibrium Analysis.

Founding neutrality of money in General Equilibrium Analysis

Let me state at the outset: if money is merely a unit of account, if this unit of account is fully known and used alike by every economic agent – or if a quantity of some kind of money relative to some commodities, which fully defines such a unit of account, is so known – and if, finally, this unit of account is assumed by all agents to be invariant over all conceivable planning horizons, then 'money' is certainly neutral. More properly speaking, however, this statement should read: this is so if and only if…! One can prove neutrality, of course, in many other ways. But the assumptions one has to make in order to do so would be quite implausible under the present conditions of highly developed and internationally highly integrated financial markets.

Around 1960, more precisely between Archibald and Lipsey (1958)[24] and Samuelson (1968),[25] the argument for monetary neutrality started to run explicitly in general equilibrium terms. As is well-known nowadays, for given endowments of individuals and given demand functions, subject to certain, apparently very weak conditions, the existence of a competitive general equilibrium of a pure exchange economy can be proved. Or, to use the particularly lucid exposition of Arrow and Hahn, which runs in terms of (the vector of) excess demand functions, termed 'z': if we assume the existence of uniquely valued excess demand functions for each price vector (their condition F), which are, in prices, homogeneous of degree zero (condition H) and continuous (condition C), and furthermore assume Walras' Law to hold (condition W), then an equilibrium price vector for a competitive economy with a finite number of goods can be shown to exist.[26] Actually, both the continuity and the unique-valuedness of the excess demand functions and even, in a sense, Walras' Law may be very much in doubt for a monetary (financial market) economy. But ignoring this, the rough and ready argument for neutrality we formerly gave our students ran in terms of the homogeneity of degree zero of excess demand functions. Calling **p** the price vector, Arrow–Hahn write this condition as follows:[27]

> Assumption $2(H) \cdot z(\mathbf{p}) = z(\mathbf{kp})$ for all $\mathbf{p} > 0$ and $\mathbf{k} > 0$; the excess demand functions are *homogeneous of degree zero* in **p**.'

So we told our students: look, due to the homogeneity of degree zero of excess demand functions, general equilibrium only depends upon relative prices, not on 'nominal' prices as such or the 'general price level'; and since money in the long run affects only nominal prices or the general price level, it is of no consequence for general equilibrium prices. We can pursue 'real economics' and monetary economics as separate and independent exercises (the classical dichotomy). Money has only the function of determining the common multiplier of all relative prices.

Stated thus, of course, the argument is evidently circular: the 'proof' is a mere reiteration of what may be called Hume's central assumption, namely that money does not affect relative prices in the long run. Arrow and Hahn themselves are more circumspect and also more explicit. They give the following explanation for the homogeneity assumption:

> The ... assumption asserts that the actions of agents depend on the rates at which goods exchange one against another and not at all on the rate at which goods exchange against the [fictional] unit of account, in this case, bancors. This assumption should not be misunderstood. If one of the goods acts as a medium of exchange, for instance, then it, too, will have a price in terms of unit of account, and it is not asserted that the rate at which goods exchange against this particular good, the medium of exchange, is of no consequence to the decisions of economic agents.[28]

So, according to the homogeneity assumption, if correctly interpreted, money, as a medium of exchange, need not be neutral in the sense that changes in its available amount could not change prices of non-monetary goods relative to money and, therefore, possibly also between each other. What the homogeneity assumption precludes, however, is that changes in the 'amount' of money – or, better, in money and monetary credit conditions – change the perception of individuals of what the fictional unit of account is. Furthermore, such a change in perception may very well be different for different agents. This would constitute a vital type of non-neutrality.

Actually, around 1960, economists tried to prove an even stronger point. They tried to show that, even if money is held as a medium of exchange, or as an asset, it would have no effect on general equilibrium prices. Archibald and Lipsey (1958) started the discussion as a critique of Patinkin's 'real balance effect'.[29] Patinkin had argued that neutrality results only if (implausibly for the real world) a particular distribution of new money balances is initially achieved. Archibald and Lipsey, on the other hand, showed (graphically) that if individuals have an equilibrium demand for real monetary balances – this is the first crucial assumption – and also for other goods and if – second crucial assumption – we have a sequence of pure exchange economies, then any injection of money at some place in the economy will, in a sequence of temporary trading equilibria in which real goods are exchanged against money, eventually lead back to the initial ('full') equilibrium. The argument was formalized by Clower and Burstein (1960).[30] The crucial point is, of course, that there is no production at temporary disequilibrium prices which would change 'endowments', or, alternatively, that we have to assume equal homothetic preferences for all individuals – a handy but, of course, vastly unrealistic assumption.

The decisive non-neutrality in the present world, however, is that exchange rates, which are largely monetarily caused, do not adjust fully to changes in general price levels in less than 12 to 15 years,[31] if at all. This changes the prices of traded relative to non-traded goods substantially. Or if it does not, and there is a large literature on the so-called pricing to markets[32] of oligopolies and incomplete 'pass-through', then profits and thus 'initial endowments' change.

But, Frank Hahn (1965) asked, why should there be an equilibrium demand for real monetary balances at all in a general economic equilibrium framework?[33] If money serves merely as a unit of account it will have an equilibrium price of zero and, if only positively valued commodities are held, nobody will actually demand it. It is extremely difficult to get around this argument and to show a positive demand for money in a full-information general equilibrium world or even in a rational expectations framework, as Hellwig showed in his presidential address.[34] However, none of this would have surprised Anacharsis the Scythian: 'If gold and silver [is] . . . of no use to the Greeks, but to assist them in numeration and arithmetic', why then should the 'Greeks' hold any amount of gold or silver at all? And, indeed, moneys serving as units of account, though actually held by no one, have been frequent in history: from the Carolingian pound and its shillings, which for centuries did not even exist physically, but were standardly used as units of account, to the equally non-existent mark of Cologne, the mark banco of Amsterdam and similar denominations in Italian city states to finally, of course, the euro, which will not exist physically before 2002, but has been a widely used unit of account since 1999. The real difficulty is that there is no necessary relationship between a unit of account and the quantity of any kind of medium of exchange, a problem glossed over by Hume and then again and again in the discussion.

What is perhaps more original in Hahn is the demonstration at the article's very end[35] that if monetary conditions cause bankruptcies, excess demand functions will not be continuous, and the general equilibrium proof breaks down for that reason. So that would be another kind of non-neutrality of money though, I believe, most of the time, that is, apart from very severe crises, nowadays not the most important one.

Samuelson (1968) concluded the theoretical discussion on monetary neutrality of the late fifties and the sixties. His aim is: 'We should be able to *prove rigorously* what is probably intuitively obvious [?] – doubling all *M* will exactly double *all* long run prices and values.'[36] He points out that in order to integrate monetary theory he was probably the first to put money – in the *Foundations*[37] – into the utility function. But he is no longer satisfied with this. He thinks that in order 'to include explicitly the quantitative convenience of money and to take into account the peculiar homogeneity properties of money resulting from the fact that its usefulness is in proportion to the scale of prices',[38] what the classical authors thought about money is best expressed by two (sets of) equations, labelled by Samuelson (A) and (B). Equation set G_i in (A) is a set of utility functions with – and I condense his notation – the vector **q** for all quantities, including factor quantities, r for the (common or average) rate of time preference, **p** for the vector of all prices, including factor prices, finally M, the quantity of money. Thus, equation set (A) reads:

$$(A)\ G_i = (\mathbf{q}, r, \mathbf{p}/M)$$

Samuelson adds equation (B), thus:

$$(B)\ M = \bar{M}, \text{ an exogenous supply}$$

This way of writing the equilibrium conditions shows up the problems of this road to 'proving' neutrality particularly clearly. There are three problems with it:

First, it is a very strong assumption that the given M in (B) is the same as that assumed by agents to be relevant in their utility functions G_i. In the spirit of Hume, we could term this the *Anacharsis assumption*.

Second, in integrated international financial markets, 'M' – or what might pass for it – is certainly not given exogenously and, in fact, it is quite unclear what it is at any moment, different individuals having at the same time quite different notions about it. Hume, at his time, might still have been of the opinion that money was a well defined quantity. In his time, Great Britain was already effectively on the gold standard. So one might have thought it was just the amount of gold in the country. Actually, as any reader of *Tom Jones* will know,[39] this narrow conception of money was not correct even then, as people were widely using commercial bills instead of 'cash' for fear of highwaymen. On the other hand, Hume was quite explicit, as is well known, that the quantity of his kind of money was not exogenous: it depended on the balance of trade (this is his legendary specie flow mechanism, most appropriate too in an internationally integrated world). Nowadays, as money – or such a near substitute to it as makes no difference – is just a sum of debt titles by many private individuals, in particular banks and credit card companies, and as it makes no difference whether you actually pay in yen, in US-dollars or in euro (though, of course, their relative prices change from day to day) nobody can tell what the amount of world money is at any moment.

The *third problem* is that equation set (A) is still incomplete. Samuelson prides himself on including *r*, the rate of time preference, in his utility functions. In fact, he tells us: 'In particular, correct neo-classical theory does not lead to the narrow anti-Keynesian view of those Chicago economists who allege that velocity of circulation is not a function of interest rates'.[40] But once we step beyond a purely static framework, and that is all to the good in monetary analysis, we must not assume that *M* will remain statically constant. In addition to *r*, the rate of time preference, we would thus have to include the rates of change of money over time – and even if we are overly modest, at least that for the next period, call it $\Delta M/M$. But this is something conceptionally quite different from *r*: it is an advance estimation of a future development; and why should all individuals have the same estimation? And thus we arrive at what may be the central point: you cannot set up your neutrality conditions in a financial markets world statically, that is, without including expectations.

Samuelson concludes his article with a tell-tale remark. He says that – apart from (A) and (B) – there was a third assumption in the classical mind: 'It was a belief in unique long run equilibrium independent of actual conditions'.[41] Exactly! This condition is essential when you admit, as Hume does, and Friedman reiterates, that money is not neutral in the short run, while asserting at the same time that it will be so in the long run. This condition is nothing but the price theory of Diocletian in the garb of Adam Smith's natural price assumption: 'The natural price ... is ... the central price to which the prices of all commodities are continually gravitating'.[42] It has been the main argument of this text, and one that I think shows the classical neutrality argument outmoded: if asset prices, including exchange rates, follow something very close to a random walk for long periods, they are neither independent of initial conditions nor do they converge; and these initial conditions depend upon perceptions of and expectations about monetary changes.

Actually, in following the price-theoretic notions about financial assets (in particular) developed in Lecture I, we can even make shorter shrift of the general equilibrium argument for neutrality: if excess demand depends not only upon prices but upon beliefs about what others think as well, solely price dependent excess demand functions do not even exist. This has been shown, among others, by Genotte and Leland[43] in their analysis of crashes, which rests explicitly on more complicated demand correspondences, not demand functions.

In fact, we may conclude the discussion in this lecture with a quotation from the Nobel Memorial Lecture of the present chief apostle of monetary neutrality: 'Hume's argument was perpetuated. The quantity-theoretic "neutrality theorems" were stated with increasing precision and worked through rigorously, using the latest equipment of static [!] general equilibrium theory. The dynamics had a kind of patched-in quality, fitting the facts, but only in a manner that suggests they could equally well fit *any* facts.'[44] If we call all beliefs of what actually constitutes money and what others are doing or going to do, and not only expectations of the future, 'dynamic', I fully agree. But even the former static General Equilibrium Theory is no longer considered 'state of the art', as further analysis in this lecture will show.

And as to the ostensibly incontrovertible facts demonstrating neutrality, I can only once more quote in full agreement from Lucas' (to my mind more than cheek-in-tongue) lecture: 'The observation that money changes induce output changes in the same direction receives confirmation in some data sets but is hard to see in others. Large-scale reductions in money growth can be associated with large-scale depressions or, if carried out in the form of credible reform, with no depression at all.'[45]

Incomplete markets, information and expectations

General equilibrium theory around 1960 tended to be static. And the ingenious idea of Arrow-Debreu securities, contingent upon future states of nature, had made it basically static even for the case of 'uncertainty' – more precisely speaking, of riskiness – of the future. By and by it became clear, however, that considering the manifold possible developments, particularly of financial markets and the length of their planning horizons, even a spanning condition for available futures contracts would most likely not be satisfied. It was recognized that we have to live – and ever more so, with more and more international capital flows – in a world of incomplete markets. Different degrees of information and expectations, possibly expectations of an interpersonally divergent nature, tended more and more to be incorporated into analysis, not least also into general equilibrium and rational expectations analysis. Finally, nominal contracts were at last incorporated into general equilibrium models. All this has wrought havoc with the assumption of the long-run neutrality of money. It is curious that this has not been realized at all by the general run of authors in discussions of the basic principles of monetary policy where, in fact, the assumption of the long-run neutrality of money has apparently been ever more securely enthroned.

A brief aside on the term 'neutrality' of money may be in place. The discussion of this topic was actually more advanced in the 1930s than it was around 1970. From the latter half of the 1970s onward we have only been regaining territory lost in between. To the best of my knowledge the term 'neutrality' of money even originated in discussions among the Austrians, in particular with Mises and Hayek and authors close to them like J.G. Koopmans or W. Egle, in the 1930s. It does not appear in Irving Fisher, *The Theory of Interest* (1907), where the (neutral) Fisher effect is extensively discussed;[46] nor does it occur in Marshall's *Principles*. If the term 'neutrality of money' had been used at all by some author before, it certainly only became prevalent by way of the Austrians. But their aim of analysis was quite different from what it is now: neutrality of money was thought to be a desirable aim for monetary policy, but one very difficult to achieve, and in particular difficult to achieve precisely. It was not thought of as the necessary long-run consequence of all monetary changes. There is a very precise, and very short, article by Hayek (1933) with 'neutrality of money' in its title.[47] And there he points out the many hurdles to be circumvented in its way. In particular, nominally fixed contracts play an important role in this article. The critics of Robert Lucas' original story[48] would have had a much easier job if they had just looked up that article of Hayek's and modelled one after the other of his counterarguments against neutrality. But unfortunately that little article was not 'available' to the then American public because it was written in German and remained untranslated.

Today, Lucas' article of 1972 is perhaps considered the decisive modern proof of neutrality, even in a framework of incomplete markets. If read correctly, though, it is the death knell of this concept. As is so well known, it runs in terms of 'second period' shocks, both real and monetary, against which one cannot insure oneself by futures contracts. The estimation problem in equilibrium pricing is how to decompose the variance due to stochastic shocks into its monetary and its 'real' component. If the change in money is exactly known, this can be done easily and money is neutral. Not so if the size of the monetary shock is unknown. It was then suggested in the popular reception of the Lucas article that under US conditions the monetary shock is always precisely known: every Thursday the Federal Reserve announces the change in base money and this is reported by every important newspaper. But this argument is both extremely atavistic and very much America-centred: atavistic because it assumes that base money (or at least M_1) is the only means of payment, as if we were still living in a cash economy where gold coin is the only acceptable money. Actually, in international financial markets you 'pay' both with privately created credit instruments and with many different national 'moneys'. The reception of Lucas' article is excessively USA-centred because it creates the impression that only local, that is, US monetary developments are of relevance; and vice versa for other countries. As one can see from empirical analyses of exchange rates this is actually true for the US-dollar, but not for other big currencies: the dollar–Deutsche Mark exchange rate, for example, depends upon a leading business cycle indicator for the USA, but not upon that for Germany, etc.[49] Thus for most countries, the relevant '*M*' is some complex index of international financial market conditions, and especially also of the US-dollar, and certainly not only one's own base money or even M_1. Therefore, monetary shocks are in general not known sufficiently closely, and – exactly according to Lucas – money is not neutral.

There is a further difficulty with the 'basic monetarist certainties'. Ordinarily, in empirical analysis, especially of exchange rates, a time series of money is used, and not one of an appropriate price level. This is rationalized by the assumption that it is money which causes, or at least will by and by cause in a forecastable way, changes in prices, so that one can use the easily available statistics of money just as well as those of prices. But the variance of changes in money is much larger than that of changes in price levels, in spite of the fact that, according to Lucas, it should be exactly the other way round. (Remember all those real shocks.) My explanation is: either reversals of temporary, politically unintended changes in money are generally expected,[50] which already entails a complicated exercise in the estimation of future policy or, even more likely, changes in money are taken as a signal for changes in financial market conditions which are themselves difficult to estimate.[51] In particular, money changes are used as an indicator for the change in asset prices of those types of assets which have no stable equilibrium price. Because of this, money is not neutral.

From about 1981 onwards, and probably largely as a reaction against Lucas (1972) and the 'rational expectations revolution', more precisely his assumption of a unique monetary equilibrium to the economy, a veritable avalanche of articles set in, all of which explicitly concluded that money was not neutral. In a sense they were all formalizations, and more explicit and elaborate restatements, of the monetary ideas of Keynes; for, if anything, the Keynes of the *General Theory* (1936), in particular chapters 12 and 13, was decidedly a non-rational-expectations theorist.[52] It is an irony of the recent history of economic thought that just when the viability of Keynesian (fiscal) policy was considered to be at its ebb, the inspiration by Keynes, the (monetary) theoretician, seemed to reach the high-water mark. Actually, this is as it should be with integrated financial markets: fiscal effects mainly go out of the window via changes in the current account while financial expectations matter. All such analysis assumes, of course, 'incomplete' financial markets.

With Azariadis[53] the tidal wave of 'sunspot' models started, and in the same year (1981) Stiglitz and Weiss[54] presented a model of equilibrium credit rationing now thought to be most convincing. The first type of argument shows that with a sufficiently high rate of time preference, a monetary economy has multiple equilibria, depending upon generally held expectations. Credit rationing, on the other hand, means that banks are quite uncertain how the credits which they give will actually be used and that the probability of default of the debtor rises with the rate of interest so that, at a certain point, it no longer pays the bank to raise interest and it cuts off further credit instead. In terms of general equilibrium theory, credit rationing theory reasons that excess demand functions are not uniquely valued and that credit markets need not necessarily clear at some price (interest rate).

I am not sure what these two so extensively mined topics of analysis really mean. The macroeconomic consequences of credit rationing have never been made clear. It is only with the precise Stiglitz–Weiss modelling, where a certain percentage of completely identical potential customers for credit are turned away, that more liberal provision of credit by the monetary authorities to the banks will reduce credit rationing and thus have real effects. But this is only due to the particular modelling technique of 'equilibrium' rationing, which frantically tries to picture credit awarded or not awarded in such a way that the goods in question are of exactly the same quality. Real-world credit rationing means much rather that a given customer does not get as much credit as he desires; or that certain classes of (potential) debtors are turned away altogether. In this case the (potential) debtors not served might be substantially submarginal, from the viewpoint of the banks. And as credits, once granted, may not be easily recallable at short notice, or more precisely recallable only at considerable cost, all customers already served may be submarginal if the expectations of the bank have worsened in that it expects a generally greater probability of default. In such a 'kinked' supply situation where the bank would very much rather reduce its outstanding credit but finds it too costly to do so, additional credit by the central bank may have no effect whatsoever. This seems to be the present Japanese situation: Japanese banks receive money practically at zero cost, but instead of using it at home they immediately invest it in the form of safe credits abroad. So what credit rationing then means is that the central bank cannot change the money supply, at least not M_1: attempts to increase it are immediately reversed by the 'destruction' of money, which goes abroad. In this case the zero change in money is 'neutral' *because* it is zero.

It is suggested in the sunspot literature, on the other hand, that monetary policy can have strong, non-neutral effects, because it can 'choose' a 'better' equilibrium among the non-unique manifold. Once more I think the actual significance is mis-stated, and mis-stated because it assumes much too great an amount of knowledge on the part of the 'authorities'. What expectational effects, to my mind, really mean is that it is quite uncertain what effects monetary policy will have. Money is non-neutral, but it is difficult to assess in what way it is so. It matters less what the central bank actually does than what it is perceived to be doing. It is much more in the business of expectation creation, of signalling and of creating and exploiting its credibility.[55]

A further piece of explicitly neutrality-denying analysis which received much attention and entailed many other similar articles[56] was that of Kiyotaki and Wright in 1989.[57] According to this seminal article – basically only an extended example – it matters very much who trades with whom and who is willing to use money in transactions and, as a store of purchasing power, between transactions. But this is more a demonstration of the real value of money as compared with a pure barter economy, which nobody would ever have denied. What it probably means for our present world is that the introduction of the euro was a non-neutral monetary change. But that was generally appreciated, and the conclusion is therefore unsurprising.

All these were fully established points basically already well known to monetary economists. There are, however, three important articles which established important new reasons for the non-neutrality of money, not intuitively understood before then.

The first is by Allen and Gale (1994):[58] their model assumes very realistically that participation in a given financial market is limited because of fixed information costs (set-up costs) to be expended if one wishes to enter a given market. Participation decisions have to be taken in advance. Furthermore, there is both a liquid and riskless financial asset (cash) and a risky asset, which has to be held for an extended period but then promises a stochastic return (i.e. stocks or bonds). Investors are differently risk-averse and therefore have different liquidity preferences. Furthermore, investors do not know in advance whether they will wish to consume little or much and early or later. In this case there may be underpricing of the risky financial asset which is auctioned if there is little liquidity in the market, where underpricing means prices are lower than the discounted future cash flow.[59] This ingenious way of showing the effect of liquidity constraints on financial markets points to two kinds of non-neutral effects of money: by 'cheapening' liquidity (that is, making credit more easily available or at lower short-term interest) monetary policy could raise the average ('real') price of financial assets and at the same time reduce price volatility.

Non-linear and nominally fixed contracts and wealth effects

The next two articles to be discussed show up the importance of the type of contracts for the real effects of changes in the amount of money as well as for changes in the financial markets in the widest sense. Bowman and Faust (1997)[60] have demonstrated that additional financial contracts which depend on prices in a non-linear way may change existing equilibria. In particular they examine options which evidently are such contracts:

> Even the fact that existing markets are complete and support a unique equilibrium is not sufficient to guarantee that a new option market will

> be redundant. If a unique risk-neutral pricing measure exists before a new option market is introduced, this measure need not be unique after the market has been introduced.[61] . . . Rather than insure against preexisting risk, option markets can create new sources of risk against which agents wish to insure themselves.[62]

The authors are mainly concerned with options while pointing out that their results are actually more general. It is easy to see that in integrated capital markets their results are also true for flexible exchange rates: for according to uncovered interest parity the change in the logarithm of the exchange rate (a non-linear function) depends on a relative price, the international difference in interest rates. Thus monetary changes which change the exchange rate regime are likely to be non-neutral. Or, to put it much more simply: changes in Exchange Rate Regimes are well known to change real exchange rate volatility; and with risk averse agents changes in volatility will change relative prices.[63]

Perhaps the most fundamental conclusions have been derived by Magill and Quinzii (1992).[64] They develop a general equilibrium model with incomplete markets and nominal assets (denominated in money) and then assume the quantity theory of money to hold. The authors account for both transaction and especially store-of-value demand for money by assuming necessarily different time points at which goods can be sold and purchased and assume different endowments of individuals (i.e. a no representative agent model). They derive a locally unique equilibrium which depends on the amount of money. If money is held as a store of value there are real effects to monetary changes regardless of whether markets are complete or incomplete, otherwise only if they are incomplete. In the Festschrift for Debreu Hens summarizes their conclusions as follows:[65]

> Equilibria are now parametrized by the monetary policy of choosing some levels of money supplies. Changing monetary policy will then have real effects . . . That is to say, even though agents are perfectly rational – i.e. they can correctly anticipate equilibrium prices as well as changes in monetary policy – still monetary policy is not neutral! It affects the means by which agents can contract on financial markets in a non-trivial way. This is definitely an innovation *vis-à-vis* the old discussion of the neutrality of money.

Nothing need be added to this statement, apart from pointing out that in a later article Magill and Quinzii (1996) showed that nominal assets in zero net supply (debt instruments) may cause speculative bubbles and then, with incomplete markets, will have real effects as well.

So, by now the general equilibrium literature lends no support at all to the assumption of the neutrality of money. Recent political literature, on the other hand, has – in a kind of pincer movement – also tended to argue for monetary non-neutrality, but in a new way: increases in money do not increase, but rather reduce, economic activity in the short run. (We could call this negative, in contrast to positive, non-neutrality.) Little conclusive evidence has been found for the assertion that a higher rate of inflation causes serious inefficiencies, as it usually goes hand-in-hand with larger deviations of somewhat sticky prices from true equilibrium prices, or because there is more confusion of agents about true equilibrium prices. Typically, these effects appear small for real economic growth, while, on the other hand, growth shifts the size of the financial sector considerably.[66] More convincing has been the reiterated message of Martin Feldstein[67] that inflation is negatively non-neutral because entrepreneurs are taxed nominally and cannot fully write off their capital assets in real terms when inflation increases their replacement cost relative to historical cost. But if taxation increases with inflation, such non-neutrality would not even have surprised David Hume.

Even the formerly secure haven of monetary neutrality, open economy macroeconomics based on foresightful (rational expectations) representative agent behaviour, has by now come up with 'the long-run nonneutrality of money'.[68] If monopolistic competition and sticky nominal prices are embodied in a model of global macroeconomic dynamics, permanent wealth, capital movement and current account effects arise. This was only to be expected by inverting the no-production-logic of the original Archibald and Lipsey demonstration.[69] Obstfeld and Rogoff note that in their model all monetary 'shocks have permanent effects on the difference between home and foreign per capita consumption . . . A positive home money shock generates a long-run improvement in the home terms of trade because it leads to an increase in wealth'.[70] They conclude: 'the possibility that money shocks may have long-lasting real effects would seem to be quite general, and not simply an artifact of this particular model. As long as there exists any type of short-run nominal rigidities, unanticipated money shocks are likely to lead to international capital flows. The resulting transfers will extend the real effects of the shock beyond the sticky-price time horizon.'[71]

Thus, neutrality of money has become an interesting metaphor which does not stand up to more general rigorous analysis, and nothing more.

Do Walras' Law and budget constraints provide a firm basis?

We have seen that even within the framework of General Equilibrium Analysis proofs for the long-run neutrality of money break down. To return to the simple conditions for equilibrium in a pure exchange economy, excess demand functions need not be uniquely valued because of credit rationing and liquidity problems, they need not be continuous because of bankruptcies, and they need not be homogeneous of degree zero because the real and the nominal components in prices cannot be disentangled; and all these aspects are monetary phenomena. In fact, unique excess demand functions may not even exist if beliefs of others are important. With nominal contracts (real) equilibrium may be parametrized in terms of the money created, even if money has only the simple function assumed in the quantity equation; and wealth effects may propagate short-term adjustment effects.

But what about Walras' Law? Writing it with the symbols used by Arrow and Hahn (1971)[72] it says that for *all* prices within the price space:

$$\mathbf{pz}(\mathbf{p}) = 0$$

After all, this is nothing but the budget constraint, that limitation imposed on all economics by scarcity, independently of the problems of information or volition. Although, to my knowledge, this has not been brought out in the literature, I think Walras' Law is nevertheless highly problematic for the case of financial asset markets.

The key aspect here is that the time point of contract formulation and that of contract solution, or payment, are generally different. Even 'spot' transactions in financial markets require payment only after the 'eternity' of a full two business days. Of course, there is no free lunch; in that sense Walras' Law holds. But there is one realization of Walras' Law *ex ante* when the contract is concluded, and in general 'another' when payment is attempted – 'another' in the sense that in general the price vector will then be different. With incomplete financial markets agents will assume certain prices of financial assets, in particular of their own assets, which turn out not to be the ones imagined in payment. Certain types of payments may, for example, not be acceptable to the other party or only at different prices from the agents' estimation; the agent may not get credit for the payment desired from his bank, etc. Derivatives, depending as they do on the variance of price movements, may have highly variable and – in more or less efficient markets – unforecastable values. Both our *ex ante* assumptions and the *ex post* financial conditions will generally depend on the prevailing monetary conditions, and in this sense 'money' may prove far from neutral.

But it is not only prices which may be quite different *ex post* and *ex ante*. It is that the goods vector need not be fully specified beforehand. Is it not likely that in many sales concluded one party will create – and both parties agree on – a debt instrument nobody had ever thought of before? Or that non-payment of a sum due may willy-nilly create another such financial asset: the claim to be paid at a later date? Thus one may circumvent the budget constraint, be it temporary or intertemporal: what one expected the constraint to be *ex ante* is not what it turns out to be *ex post*. Strictly speaking, the budget constraint need not even hold eventually, as non-payment or partial payment may occur. The admissible *ad hoc* creation of financial assets by contracting individuals may have much to do with conditions of monetary stringency or liquidity. And such contracting and recontracting can be of real importance for the world economy, as the history of Long-Term Capital Management and its successful restructuring by the intermediation of the Federal Reserve have shown.[73]

I repeat that the non-neutral effects of a given type of the many kinds of money in international financial markets depend much more on perceptions and on interpretations of what has happened and on expectations thereby created than on what tangible changes really take place. One can see that from exchange rates which are, after all, only internationally valid market prices of one money against the other: even the two exchange rates between the 'Big three' – US-dollar, euro and yen – will on quite normal market days change by one half per cent to perhaps 2 per cent a day; and during only three days in October 1998 the yen appreciated against the dollar by a full 20 per cent. It is hard to believe that real shocks are that large or that frequent, in particular as demand for foreign exchange cannot be very inelastic. On the face of it there appears to be 'excess volatility'.[74] Much more appropriately, though, one would say that international financial assets are without a stable equilibrium price.

I close by returning to martingale behaviour, and martingales in the logarithms of the price, as typical for financial market assets in general and exchange rates in particular. In this case financial shocks have permanent effects. Future prices cannot be said to become systematically different in the mean from the present one. There is no 'mean reversion' and no forecastability of prices. Then, short-run non-neutrality *is* long-run non-neutrality.

As long as monetary theory, and above all policy, is centred on the neutrality of money it does not take notice either of palpable empirical facts or of what has gone on in financial market theory and in exchange rate theory. Those apparently isolated by the comforting fence of monetary neutrality have not realized that neutrality has been theoretically dismantled on the other side, and in many ways, especially so in exchange rate empirics and theory. Money is non-neutral because it is not only a numéraire, as Anacharsis the Scythian in Hume's story believed. And even if it were only a numéraire it would be one of a not sufficiently determinate value depending on subjective judgements about the amounts of monetary assets in existence.

Notes

1 Can anyone believe that a 70 per cent appreciation of the yen against the euro within two years since October 1998 and a 35 per cent appreciation of the dollar against the euro within one and three quarter years are, considering the well-known prevalence of hysteresis on European economic relations, without real effects even for the longer run?

2 See Neumann (1995), op. cit., Lecture III, note 14.

3 How times change: during the First Congress of the International Economic Association, or 43 years earlier, Gottfried Haberler – as far away as anyone can be from Keynesianism, much rather a prototypical Quasi-Monetarist of the Austrian variety and the progenitor of that effect 'named after Pigou but developed by Haberler', which the textbooks seem to consider a linchpin of monetary neutrality – argued quite unabashedly, though cautiously, in non-neutrality terms:

> Monetary factors, comprehensively defined, bear a heavy share of responsibility for short-run economic instability [so far, of course, standard, but here it comes:] . . . If it is true that monetary factors greatly contribute to economic instability, does it follow that they adversely influence economic growth? Not necessarily. . . . We thus reach the conclusion that monetary factors . . . may help as well as hinder economic progress; but it is easier to think of authentic and dramatic cases of the latter than the former.

Gottfried Haberler, 'Monetary Factors Affecting Economic Stability', in: D.C. Hague (ed.), *Stability and Progress in the World Economy*, London 1958, pp. 151–78, quotations from pp. 175–8. The following sentence may serve as a motto for what I wish to say: 'I conclude that the response mechanism is more important than the severity of the external shocks; and in the response mechanism monetary factors play a most important rôle' (ibid. p. 177).

4 J.M. Keynes, *The General Theory of Employment Interest and Money*, London 1936, p. 167.

5 John Locke, *Some Considerations of the Consequences of the Lowering of Interest, and Raising the Value of Money*, London 1692.

6 Richard Cantillon, *Essai sur la nature du commerce en général* [supposedly] London, 1755, originally English.

7 Karl Marx *Das Kapital* (1867/1967), p. 520.

8 Cantillon, op. cit., Part II, ch. 3–10, in particular ch. 6.

9 Cantillon, op. cit., Part II, ch. 10: mere 'rumour' is important in changing the rate of interest.

10 The importance of Hume's original ideas on neutrality is fully recognized in Robert E. Lucas, Jr., 'Nobel Lecture: Monetary Neutrality', *Journal of Political Economy*, 104 (1996), 661–82.

11 David Hume, *Political Discourses*, Edinburgh 1752, Discourse IV, 'Of Interest', 61–78, here pp. 61ff.

12 Smith, *Inquiry into the Nature and Causes of the Wealth of Nations* (1776), II.ii.26: 'The substitution of paper in the room of gold and silver money, replaces a very expensive instrument of commerce with one much less costly, and sometimes equally convenient.'

13 Hume (1752), op. cit., Discourse III, 'Of Money', p. 43.

14 Hume ibid. p. 40.

15 Hume ibid. p. 46.

16 In fact, doubts about 'superneutrality' seem to be no longer the fashion among the most orthodox. Lucas (1996), op. cit. says (p. 665): 'The central (!) predictions of the quantity theory are that, in the long run, money growth (!) should be neutral in its effects on the growth rate of production and should affect the inflation rate on a one-for-one basis.'

17 Milton Friedman, 'The Role of Monetary Policy', *American Economic Review*, 58 (1968), 1–17, here p. 10.

18 See p. 132.

19 It is just now being translated into English by an Institute of the Austrian Academy of Sciences. See Carl Menger, 'Geld', *Handwörterbuch der Staatswissenschaften*, vol. III, Jena 1892, pp. 730–57; 2nd edn: vol. IV, Jena 1900, pp. 60–106; 3rd edn: vol. IV, Jena 1909, pp. 555–610; the last named version republished in *The Collected Works of Carl Menger*, F.A. Hayek (ed.), vol. IV, London 1936, pp. 1–116.
20 Menger (1936), op. cit., vol. IV, p. 110.
21 Friedrich von Wieser, *Theorie der gesellschaftlichen Wirtschaft*, Grundriss der Sozialökonomik I/2, 2nd edn, Tübingen 1924, §49, p. 186: 'Massengewohnheit der Verwendung', more usually quoted as 'Massengewohnheit der Annahme'.
22 Haberler (1958), op. cit., p. 177.
23 Don Patinkin, *Money, Interest, and Prices – An Integration of Monetary and Value Theory*, New York 1956, 2nd edn, 1965.
24 G.C. Archibald and R.G. Lipsey, 'Monetary and Value Theory: A Critique of Lange and Patinkin', *Review of Economic Studies*, 26 (1958), 1–22.
25 Paul A. Samuelson, 'What Classical and Neoclassical Monetary Theory Really Was', *Canadian Journal of Economics*, 1 (1968), 1–15.
26 Kenneth J. Arrow and Frank H. Hahn, *General Competitive Analysis,* San Francisco–Edinburgh 1971, pp. 18–28.
27 Ibid. p. 19.
28 Ibid. p. 19. My only criticism: perhaps it would have been better to have said: 'the actions of agents depend on the rates at which goods *are known* to exchange one against each other'.
29 See Patinkin (1956), op. cit.
30 Robert Clower and M.L. Burstein, 'On the Invariance of Demand for Cash and Other Assets', *Review of Economic Studies*, 28 (1960), 32–6.
31 Kenneth S. Rogoff, 'The Purchasing Power Parity Puzzle', *Journal of Economic Literature*, 32 (1996), 647–68. James R. Lothian and Mark P. Taylor, 'Real Exchange Rate Behavior: The Recent Float from the Perspective of the Past Two Centuries', *Journal of Political Economy*, 104 (1996), 488–509. (As always I take adjustment up to where only a 5 per cent deviation remains as the measuring rod, not the unambitious measure of the 'half-life'.)
32 Among many, see especially the pertinent papers by Michael Knetter, e.g. 'International Comparison of Pricing-to-Market Behavior', *American Economic Review*, 83 (1993), 473–86.
33 Frank H. Hahn, 'On Some Problems of Proving the Existence of an Equilibrium in a Monetary Economy', in: F.H. Hahn and F.P.R. Brechling (eds), *The Theory of Interest Rates*, New York 1965, pp. 126–35.
34 Martin F. Hellwig, 'The Challenge of Monetary Theory', *European Economic Review*, 37 (1993), 215–42.
35 Hahn (1965), op. cit., pp. 132ff.
36 Samuelson (1968), op. cit., p. 5.
37 Paul A. Samuelson, *Foundations of Economic Analysis*, Cambridge, MA 1948.
38 Ibid. p. 10, in italics.
39 When he sends him off to London to start a new life, Squire Allworthy provides Tom Jones not with a bag of guineas, but with a commercial bill of five hundred pounds. Henry Fielding, *Tom Jones, or the History of a Foundling*, London 1759. For less anecdotal evidence see T.S. Ashton, *An Economic History of England: The 18th Century*, London 1955, pp. 185ff.
40 Samuelson (1968), op. cit., p. 11.
41 Ibid. p. 11f.
42 Smith (1776), I.vii.15.
43 Genotte and Leland (1990), op. cit., Lecture VI, note 17.
44 Lucas (1996), op. cit., pp. 668f.

45 Ibid. p. 668.
46 Irving Fisher, *The Theory of Interest – Its Nature, Determination and Relation to Economic Phenomena*, New York 1907, pp. 78ff.
47 F.A. Hayek, 'Über "neutrales" Geld', *Zeitschrift für Nationalökonomie*, 4 (1933), 659–61. Hayek also names authors who used the term 'neutrality' of money simultaneously with him.
48 Robert E. Lucas, Jr., 'Expectations and the Neutrality of Money', *Journal of Economic Theory*, 4 (1972), 103–24.
49 See Wolfgang Pohn, *Do U.S. and German Business Cycles Explain the Mark/Dollar Exchange Rate?*, Master's thesis, University of Vienna, 2000.
50 Bennet T. McCallum, 'A Reconsideration of the Uncovered Interest Parity Relationship', *Journal of Monetary Economics*, 33 (1994), 105–32.
51 See the discussion in Lecture V, p. 96f.
52 The entire argument on the speculation motive assumes that some individuals think they are better informed than the 'market', in other words that the financial markets are *not* considered efficient in the modern sense.
53 Costas Azariadis, 'Self-Fulfilling Prophecies', *Journal of Economic Theory*, 25 (1981), 380–96.
54 Joseph E. Stiglitz and Andrew Weiss, 'Credit Rationing in Markets with Imperfect Information', *American Economic Review*, 71 (1981), 393–410.
55 Alex Cukierman, Sebastian Edwards and Guido Tabellini, 'Seignorage and Political Instability', *American Economic Review*, 82 (1992), 537–55.
56 See, e.g. S. Rao Aiyagari and Neil Wallace, 'Existence of Steady States with Positive Consumption in the Kiyotaki–Wright Model', *Review of Economic Studies*, 58 (1991), 901–16; Nobuhiro Kiyotaki and Randall Wright, 'A Search-Theoretic Approach to Monetary Economics', *American Economic Review*, 83 (1993), 63–77; Alberto Trejos and Randall Wright, 'Search, Bargaining, Money, and Prices', *Journal of Political Economy*, 103 (1995), 118–41; Ricardo de O. Cavalcanti, Andres Erosa and Ted Tembelides, 'Private Money and Reserve Management in a Random-Matching Model', *Journal of Political Economy*, 107 (1999), 929–45.
57 Nobuhiro Kiyotaki and Randall Wright, 'On Money as a Medium of Exchange', *Journal of Political Economy*, 97 (1989), 927–54.
58 Franklin Allen and Douglas Gale, 'Limited Market Participation and Volatility of Asset Prices', *American Economic Review*, 84 (1994), 933–55.
59 Franklin Allen and Douglas Gale, 'Bubbles and Crises', *Economic Journal*, 110 (2000), 236–55, have extended their analysis of 'the equilibrium asset price *P* (being) at least as high as the fundamental price *P*' (p. 245) to bank credit financing of risky assets.
60 David Bowman and Jon Faust, 'Options, Sunspots, and the Creation of Uncertainty', *Journal of Political Economy*, 105 (1997), 957–75.
61 Ibid. p. 958f.
62 Ibid. p. 958.
63 See Neumann (1995), op. cit., Lecture III, note 14.
64 Michael J.P. Magill and Martine Quinzii, 'Real Effects of Money in General Equilibrium', *Journal of Mathematical Economics*, 21 (1992), 301–42.
65 Thorsten Hens, 'Incomplete Markets' in: A. Kirman (ed.), *Elements of General Equilibrium Analysis* (dedicated to Gérard Debreu for his 75th birthday), Oxford 1998, ch. 5, pp. 139–210.
66 Peter N. Ireland, 'Money and Growth: An Alternative Approach', *American Economic Review*, 83 (1993), 47–65.
67 Martin Feldstein, 'Inflation, Income Taxes, and the Rate of Interest: A Theoretical Analysis', *American Economic Review*, 66 (1976), 809–20; and 'The Costs and Benefits of Going from Low Inflation to Price Stability', in:

Christina D. Romer and David H. Romer, *Reducing Inflation – Motivation and Strategy*, Chicago and London 1997, ch. 3, pp. 123–66.
68 Obstfeld and Rogoff (1995), op. cit., p. 644, Lecture V, note 9.
69 See Archibald and Lipsey (1958), op. cit., and the discussion in this lecture, p. 128.
70 Obstfeld and Rogoff (1995), op. cit., p. 639, p. 643.
71 Ibid. p. 644.
72 Arrow and Hahn (1971), op. cit., p. 21.
73 See Franklin R. Edwards, 'Hedge Funds and the Collapse of Long-Term Capital Management', *Journal of Economic Perspectives*, 13/2 (Spring 1999), 189–210.
74 Robert J. Shiller, 'Do Stock Prices Move Too Much to be Justified by Subsequent Changes in Dividends?', *American Economic Review*, 71 (1981), 421–36.

Index